D1507811

if these
walls
could talk

{
a therapist

reveals 25 stories

of change

and how they

will work

for you
}

Thomas A. Habib, Ph.D.

How to order:

U.S. Bookstores and Libraries: Please submit all orders to
Conifer Publishing
Post Office Box 131141
La Costa, California 92013

Telephone: (949) 248-7411, Ext. 101
Email: *ConiferPub@aol.com*
Internet: *www.mpccares.com/talkingwalls*

Quantity discounts are available from Conifer Publishing. Submit requests to above address on your letterhead and include the number of books and intended use.

If These Walls Could Talk

A Therapist Reveals 25 Stories of Change and How They Will Work for You

Thomas A. Habib, Ph.D.

Conifer Publishing

Conifer Publishing
Post Office Box 131141
La Costa, California 92013
(949) 248-7411, Ext. 101

Editing by	Barbara McNichol
	Barbara McNichol Editorial
Cover Copy by	Susan Kendrick
	Susan Kendrick Writing
Cover Design by	Kathi Dunn
	Dunn & Associates Design
Book Design by	Michele DeFilippo
	1106 Design

Printed in Canada

**Publisher's Cataloging-in-Publication
(Provided by Quality Books, Inc.)**
   Habib, Thomas A.
   If these walls could talk : a therapist reveals 25
stories of change and how they will work for you /
Thomas A. Habib
   p. cm.
   Includes bibliographical references and index.
   LCCN 2003096616
   ISBN 0-9727672-6-6
   1. Psychotherapy--Case studies. I. Title.
   RC465.H33 2004   616.89'14
                    QBI03-700729

Praise for
If These Walls Could Talk

Dr. Habib is a warm, bright therapist with a great sense of humor. *If These Walls Could Talk* truly offers a great deal to learn.

— *CYNTHIA HOGAN MARLBOROUGH,*
DIRECTOR OF BUSINESS DEVELOPMENT, SOUTH SHORE HOSPITAL,
SOUTH WEYMOUTH, MASSACHUSETTS

Dr. Habib's contributions to how we think about love and marriage are revolutionary. In *If These Walls Could Talk* you'll learn lessons of love that will change those subtle feelings of disappointment I've seen many couples needlessly harbor. A remarkable book by a remarkable therapist.

— *MIE LYNN TSUCHIMOTO, PSY.D.,*
CLINICAL PSYCHOLOGY

If These Walls Could Talk is a welcomed addition to the self-help literature. Dr. Habib is a psychologist who understands that sociological variables also factor into human behavior. His insights into women and men as individuals, as well as in their roles as partners and parents, are wise indeed. Count on a read that's engaging enough to inspire real change.

MEREDITH GOULD, PH.D.
SOCIOLOGIST AND AUTHOR
DELIBERATE ACTS OF KINDNESS

Disclaimer

This book is designed to provide information in regard to the subject matter covered. It is sold with the understanding that the publisher and author are not engaged in rendering professional services for you, your marriage, or family. If professional services are necessary, treatment should be sought from a clinical psychologist or a physician in your community. Local or state associations can provide guidance in acquiring a referral.

The purpose of this book is to educate and entertain. The author and Conifer Publishing shall have neither liability nor responsibility to any person or entity with respect to any adverse outcome, loss or damage caused, or alleged to be caused, directly or indirectly by the information contained in this book.

The people depicted in these stories have given explicit permission on what and how to release their stories. In every instance, names and circumstances were altered to protect confidentiality. Any similarities to other people or the author's former patients are purely coincidental. Stories were intentionally selected to have a wide range of applicability and interest.

If you do not wish to be bound by the above, you may return this book to the publisher for a full refund.

Acknowledgments

"Many people in our lives want us to succeed," I wrote at the conclusion of this book. Furthermore, I wrote that it's important to
give thanks. So I'll follow the advice I write about (something I admit
I don't always do). That is, to say thank you to all of my patients who
allowed me to share their life experiences and to the countless others who inspired many of these stories. You couldn't have known how
often the lessons learned from your valiant struggles have helped
many people I've worked with after you.

I am in debt to Christine Baser, Ph.D., R.N., my colleague and wife,
for helping me develop some of the book's central concepts. In their
earliest stages, the ideas were crude and occasionally contradictory.
Christine, I knew if I could convince you of any underlying merit
they might hold, it was prudent to continue developing them. More
than that, your written commentaries, grammatical corrections, and
encouragement were invaluable.

I give thanks to Cynthia Hogan Marlborough, for your painstaking
review, suggestions, and friendship. To Janet Parent for your honest
and tough critiques that helped me find a consistency and style that
improved the manuscript. To first-draft readers Kimberley Weimer,
Joan Bee, Mary Waltari, J.D., Helena Jacobson, Mie Lynn Tsuchimoto,
Psy.D., and Tami Tucker, Ph.D. All of you enhanced the final product and unfailingly grounded me in what the reader would perceive.
To my cousin Geraldine Cote, for your suggestions and support in
helping me remember my own past.

To Ellen Fein, Mary LoVerde, and Michelle Morris Spieker, thank you for your support and encouragement. A few words from Mary at a conference where we co-presented provided much momentum and determination for this book. We are often unaware how much we help people.

The outstanding writing and design professionals who graciously worked on this project consistently came through with their expertise. Thank you Barbara McNichol (Barbara McNichol Editorial) for your gentle style as you rescued my tortured prose from incomprehensibility. Thank you Susan Kendrick (Susan Kendrick Writing) for your fluid creativity and generosity. Thank you Michele DeFilippo (1106 Design, LLC) for your prompt and responsive production style. Thank you Kathi Dunn (Dunn & Associates) for an outstanding cover and jacket design. I would also like to thank Robin Quinn (Quinn's Word for Word) for your excellent recommendations and resources, and Shannon Bodie and Allison Wildman (Lightbourne, LLC) for your early support and education.

Know that part of all of you has been embedded in this manuscript. I believe that what we've pulled together will help many along the road we all travel.

Lucienne Marie Brisebois Habib
(1925–1973)

Table of Contents

Part 1: Introduction

There is only one river of truth,
but many streams fall into it on this side and that.

CLEMENT OF ALEXANDRIA, 190 A.D.

1

⌒⊙⌒⊙⌒

Before Closing the Doors

When you step into a therapist's office, you want to understand how your therapy will work, what to expect from your doctor, and what's expected of you. Just opening this book doesn't mean you're starting a psychotherapy session. Still, it's appropriate to provide some information, just as I do at the outset of my real-life therapy sessions.

In the role of patient, the most crucial part is that you *feel understood* in your therapy sessions. Study after study shows the importance of the psychologist hearing your experiences and understanding your perceptions. That doesn't mean your therapist agrees with every-thing you say. This may strike you as obvious—that the value of coun-sel would be lost if the therapist agreed with everything. But the process is about helping you see things in a new, at times difficult, way that provides value.

In the chapters that follow, you'll identify with stories and opin-ions that make you laugh and cry, that inspire you, that may even enrage you. If you disagree with something or feel angry about it, I hope you don't quickly dismiss it. If I were sitting with you, I would encourage you to wrestle with the emotions behind it and explore issues that evoke distress. Wrestling with your emotions can be productive and enlightening. As most clinical psychologists would say, "They're trying to tell you something." Whatever your reaction, stay open to the messages you receive in a courageous, wholehearted search for your truth.

If this were your therapy session, I'd discourage you from blindly accepting anything that's contrary to your experiences or sensibilities. Never swallow anything whole—including messages without merit from your history or even from lessons presented in this book. Take a stance similar to one you'd take with a loved one when you disagree by saying, "I hear what you're saying, but I can't see it yet. Let me think about it."

A few reviewers of an early draft of this book reacted strongly to several chapters. To be specific, in "Getting Older," I criticize cosmetic surgery and the perpetual search for the fountain of youth. In "Romantic Ideals that Hurt" and in "Minutes of Love," I take on our culture's cherished but unrealistic expectations about love. In "He Wants Sex and She Wants to be Hugged," I critique my colleagues while ruffling political sensitivities about sex and intimacy. As I revised these chapters, I used some of their excellent suggestions but chose not to exclude anything from the book solely because it might evoke anger, offend colleagues, elicit disapproval from my community of faith, or sell fewer books. The vast majority of mental health professionals believe they owe their patients an honest opinion. This is what I give you in *If These Walls Could Talk*.

Some topics in this book may not seem relevant to you. For example, if you are unmarried and without children, the chapters in Part Four: About Families and Parenthood, may hold little interest. Although reading the stories in a particular order isn't critical, I strongly encourage you to read *all* chapters so you can see how the lessons transcend the circumstances described.

You'll also see I've included assignments for you. I believe it's not enough to only gain insight into issues. To make changes in your life, you have to translate those insights into practices. Some changes need to be made over time; others involve small day-to-day practices that add up to profound changes over the years. With practice, you'll be able to translate—then implement—these insights and lessons into your life.

Certain topics may affect you intensely, so give yourself time to reflect. Remember to practice a gentle self-discipline, write in a journal, or talk about your reflections with someone you trust. Don't ignore your thoughts and feelings. As an example, many men are surprised to learn that the average woman, their wives included, will never desire to have sex as much as they do ("He Wants Sex and She Wants to be Hugged").

Reading this book may reveal an underlying depression or unearth a conflict, inspiring you to seek professional counsel. One person who reviewed this book gained insight into her desire to learn more about herself through therapy, and decided to begin. Most clinical psychologists love to work with people seeking growth. It's much easier to work with people when their lives aren't burdened by the clutter caused by crises or neglect.

I hope you benefit from the hard-gained insights graciously shared by the people I counseled. On behalf of myself and all my readers, I want to express my warm gratitude to those who have given permission to use their life stories.

Stay with me while I take you behind closed doors and share the lessons learned within my office walls.

If the doors of perception were cleansed,
we would see everything.

WILLIAM BLAKE (1757–1827)

2

Behind Closed Doors

Laurie held her breath to assure her stillness, but she'd started to hold it too soon. She stood half naked with her right breast uncomfortably squeezed between the plates of the x-ray machine. The dosage of radiation from her mammogram was less than what she would absorb sunning herself on the beach, she'd been assured. Doubt added to her discomfort when she saw the technician scurry out of the room and seek refuge behind a thickly windowed fortress. She held one more long breath before she heard the sliding shutter of the machine release its imaging rays. They penetrated her breast and made their ghostly impression on the plate beneath.

This was Laurie's third mammogram since turning 35.

The technician asked her to get dressed but remain nearby until she could verify that the plates were readable. An hour later, Laurie sat in her physician's office on the crinkly paper draping the examining table. Dr. Livingston held the x-ray in her hand and made her way to the light box hanging on the wall. She told Laurie, "Your mammogram came back and I want to re-do it."

"Oh... ," was all Laurie could manage, fighting off a wave of fear-induced nausea that struck her.

Laurie insisted on repeating the mammogram that day, not the next week. A telephone call confirmed that this was possible. So two hours later, she was back on the crinkly paper and the verdict hadn't improved. Her doctor said, "The shadow is still showing up. But I don't want you to worry. These things usually turn out to be nothing and if they are, they're more likely to be cysts or calcium deposits."

The words "the shadow was still showing up" echoed uncontrollably in her thoughts. Laurie heard very little after being told "it" was still there. Now, a darkness stalked her through this supposedly unremarkable side street down the road of life. Recollections of her mom's death from breast cancer at 42 years of age haunted her. Chatter about her older sister's radical mastectomy pierced her thoughts and quickened her pulse.

Typical of Laurie, her anger displaced fear about this crisis that came out of nowhere. Anger that this shadow interjected itself into her life at this time. After all, this visit was supposed to be routine—just another thing to get done this week. But she knew this news would consume her unless the biopsy scheduled for the next month proved negative. Earlier, she'd been in a hurry to get to work—a desire that suddenly seemed irrelevant as a blast of directionless feelings whizzed through her thoughts.

Laurie's life was being altered and she was just trying to hang on—hang on despite the disorientation she knew was coming.

Life-Defining Events

What's a life-defining event? Laurie's news certainly qualifies as one. Indeed, everyone encounters these events at some point in time. They can't be avoided. Some are frightening and others evoke joy. One way or another, the existence we come to know can, in a moment, be transformed by a loved one's death, a financial windfall, a major illness, a new relationship, a promotion, even an unexpected request for divorce. They can sweep us into unchartered waters filled with tumultuous feelings and thoughts.

The life we once led and the meaning it held changes forever when a life-defining event happens and an unplanned chapter unfolds. Life-defining events can range from a personal insight, an epiphany, to an apocalyptic tragedy—one we didn't see coming. Laurie's experience proved to be apocalyptic. Her biopsy confirmed cancer. It was followed by a mastectomy and reconstructive breast surgery, causing her to rewrite the plot in her life story. Nevertheless, Laurie was about to discover aspects of herself that would have gone unrealized.

Through these life-defining events both positive and negative, I have seen repeatedly a remarkable ability for people to transcend. Transcending isn't a matter of recapturing or returning to a former state but ending up in a desirable place they'd never achieve without experiencing hardship.

Although life isn't fair, it's possible to experience an inherent justice in outcomes of this nature. We learn that much of what we go through—often involving pain—isn't endured in vain. After her diagnosis and treatment, Laurie learned to live in a much fuller way. She once lived by assertion driven by anxiety; now she practices contentment and appreciation.

Through all the life stories heard within my office walls, I've learned to be in awe of the resiliency of the human spirit. I stand in reverence at our ability to persevere and continue, to give meaning

We learn that much of what we go through— often involving pain—isn't endured in vain.

and purpose to anything life throws our way. And through these stories, I have repeatedly witnessed the essential dignity of people to emerge stronger and nobler than ever. I would list this among a human being's finest attributes. This is the transcendence.

Limitations and the Transcendence

We live with the limitations we encounter while maintaining an awareness of the endless possibilities life offers. This statement is not a contradiction, although it's somewhat paradoxical. At any time, there are things we can have and things we can't have. It is imperative we distinguish between the two. We want to be fully available to seek what is attainable. To be ready to receive what *is* available and avoid wasting energy pursuing what isn't. To be open to special, transcendent moments.

This presents a challenge inherent in living with life's possibilities and limitations at the same time. We only need to look at our culture's resistance to letting go of youth and how we cope with getting older to feel this struggle. Aging creams, plastic surgery, hair transplants, liposuction, face-lifts, and botox injections are symbol of this struggle. We lose self-acceptance if we pursue these things. These ever-present wishes for perpetual youth, romance, sex, wealth, and power will be discussed in the chapters that follow.

My Role as a Psychologist

Through the years, people have asked me how I can listen to problems day after day, year upon year. Although I have to admit to times of emotional depletion, frustration, and doubt, I accept them as part of my work. It is also true, however, that those asking this question haven't observed the subsequent transformations in the lives of people I counsel. These results sustain me. By asking this question, perhaps they are experiencing their own fear of change, unable to remember that what begins as a tragedy usually ends as a triumph of the human spirit. This is what makes us a remarkable species. It is why I am content with my life's work. I am grateful to earn my living as a clinical psychologist.

The following chapters bring you into the consultation room to listen to the changes people have undergone. By writing them, I'm satisfying a reoccurring desire, that is, a wish that many people could sit with me and watch these transformations, knowing how enlightening certain issues could be for them in their journey through life.

In many of the chapters, I touch on transcendent moments—when the brilliant light of insight enables people to understand better; to feel awe; to see new possibilities; to let go of their frustration, pain, anger, depression; to feel content; to identify a preferred path. Through all of these stories, we draw on experiences that brought people precisely to this point. To realize truth. To find ways of living tailored to our hopes, histories, and journeys. To be ready and eager to search. To find something beyond ourselves and beyond the known.

Learning Life's Lessons

If we indeed learn more from our failures than our successes, so be it. Education has always been expensive. But I continue to believe that many of life's lessons can be acquired through personal insight and growth that comes to those seeking consciousness. The popularity of the self-help movement suggests this is becoming a reality. Personally, I prefer pursuing learning to grow while heading off as many apocalyptic transformations as possible. This is far less painful yet still contains essential truths about life-promising improvements.

Birth and death are germane to all parts of nature, which is why we're slated for our share of apocalyptic transformations. No one escapes this reality, whether it's the literal death of a living thing or the metaphorical death of a part of our lives. Life comes with limitations and real pain.

However, the cycle of death and birth is dreaded needlessly. Although change is difficult, its payoff contains wisdom and emotional growth. That which is born from tragedy often gives birth to a better life. Forests devastated by fire, valleys fertilized by flood, lives renewed by the deaths of loved ones. Yes, the phoenix does rise from the ashes; rebirth is always at hand.

Working to Live

After Laurie's radical mastectomy, she learned to live with the reality that if she was cancer free for the next five years, she'd likely beaten the disease. But Laurie didn't wait five years to live; she began living fully right away, pursuing dreams that were only an afterthought before her life-defining transformation.

What she really cared about was enjoying her marriage, finding time for friends and family, and having at least one child. (What do you care about? It's a question you may be afraid to wrestle with until it's forced upon you.) As a result, Laurie and Doug simplified their life together. They sold their home in southern California and left their jobs to move to a small town in Colorado. One might contend the jobs they took in Colorado were backward moves. Not so. Their transformation included the pivotal decision that they would *work to live*, not live to work.

They also fulfilled a meaningful desire when their little girl was born. In the yearly Christmas card Laurie sends me, I hardly recognize the face of the new mother I once knew but always warmly remember the courageous woman who chose to live her dreams.

Live well, Laurie.

Part 2: About You

Sitting quietly, doing nothing
Spring comes and the grass grows by itself.

ALLAN W. WATTS, 1957

3

Lives Without Time to Live:
Wounded Warriors

Each night, John falls asleep on the couch as the newspaper drapes his face and covers his exhausted body. Sleep is his only merciful release—a reprieve from a relentless agenda that cycles again the next morning. But even sleep has become increasingly agitated as his commitments accumulate along with his wealth.

John appears to have it all. He's admired for his achievements and what they have brought. His determination to succeed is as relentless as the pounding ocean surf he no longer has time to ride. His colleagues attribute his string of successes to the model of efficiency he embodies. John anticipates problems and opportunities with uncanny accuracy, which accounts for his rapid promotions and excellence as a senior vice president at a software company.

His pencil-filled schedule only partially traces the terrain he crosses. Day in and day out, he adapts by smoothly reacting to whatever comes his way. He maintains a cool exterior and a riveting focus on the long-range goals he's set. Despite his workweek—55 hours plus—he undertakes never-ending home improvement projects and helps his wife raise their three children. Yet although his life is chock full of the finer things that money can buy, John has no time to live it.

John called me to help him cope with what he called a stress reaction. He was suffering through what he initially feared was a heart attack. A trip to the emergency room in a blaring ambulance ruled out coronary heart disease. His diagnosis was anxiety or, more accurately, a panic attack.

John wondered if he was losing it. He was used to being in control. A panic attack seemed impossible but he knew something was definitely wrong. He felt slightly ashamed and struggled with believing extreme anxiety was the culprit.

Hard to Let Go

As the millennium begins anew, cultural influences remain strong and unyielding in the land where our collective mantra has become an absurd expectation that we must give 110%.

The completion of one task rarely is followed by a period of idleness so we have a chance to reflect, feel content, or even celebrate a job well done. Always on the go, we rush from one event to another. Measuring how much time we spend stalks our every move. We rarely question this frantic pace; we only question our inability to cope with the fatigue and anxiety that goes with it. But why do we accept this pace at all?

Many times, fear keeps us moving—a fear that's barely perceptible. Time and again I can hear the message behind this unconscious fear: if we aren't striving and working, something bad will happen. Financial failure, parental or spousal inadequacy, poor health, early aging, and so on. When we're moving, it feels right because it seems to offer renewal. We feed our precious time to the voracious monster of activity but it still demands more—never satisfied. We continue to live seduced by an illusion that the accomplishment of one more task will bring feelings of security or completeness. Only once it's totally finished can we rest. Yet rest-time never comes.

Running a few steps ahead feeling like a failure keeps John (and many of us) on this frantic treadmill. Without careful thought about what we want in our daily agenda, we become weighed down with new obligations. On and on we pursue vaguely defined goals—the accumulation of wealth, the acquisition of more things, and so on. We set our automatic pilot to accept any possibility. Then we become obligated to the series of tasks that follow. It becomes a frenetic journey unguided by purpose and thus without destination. We invest our efforts to guard against vague fears of trouble or threat. We sense a need to keep moving, keep pushing.

Why does John's life (and our lives) become burdened with commitments? Because some time during our childhood or teen years, we swallowed the absurd notion that "we can have it all." We only need to watch television to observe the daily dose of tantalizing images suggesting "we can have it all." Because we want to believe that's achievable, we devote enormous time and energy to pursuing this ideal—without fully knowing or consenting to what it takes. Does it give us time to contemplate? To be with the people who matter? To put aside goal-directed activities? No. Instead, the relentlessness of purposeful activity drains us. We don't know how to live without these compulsions.

Think about being on a long vacation and losing track of time, when you forget, even momentarily, what day of the week it is. Vacations illustrate a compulsion-free style in which being absorbed in the events of your vacation define your life rather than your wristwatch or "to do" list.

Did we absorb too much of the cultural message about needing to have financial resources? Isn't owning a large stock portfolio supposed to make all the anxiety pay off? Is rushing from one obligation to another really worthwhile? For Laurie who had breast cancer, financial gain wasn't worth the hectic lifestyle. A few months after John started seeing me, he decided it wasn't worth it, either.

Is there another path to take, at least some of the time? There is, but first more information on why we take one that allows us no time to live.

Ignore Cultural Messages

Some powerful cultural influences set many on paths not unlike John's. We live in a country that deifies the economic model of relentless capitalism. A central tenet of its creed is "if you're not producing, you will be replaced."

Constant change reaffirms this tenet. Consider these: new fashions, obsolescence in durable goods, and a culture at war with itself over aging. Loyalty and continuity have diminishing value. The message is: "You're only as good as your last attempt."

Capitalism is an economic model, not a template upon which we should live our lives. Although capitalism appears to be the best model to improve economic wealth, it's not clear at what point we become slaves to its demands. The competition we feel creates anxiety and feelings of insecurity. We try harder and become even more committed to compensate until exhaustion results. "Even after the end of the day, I don't feel content," John told me in our discussions. I could feel the exhaustion he hid beneath his ambition and perseverance. Therefore, like John, we must each decide where to draw the line in our consumer-oriented society and ignore cultural messages that direct our lives.

Other sources of anxiety prompt us to feed the beast. For John, they originated with a family that was economically frail. In our discussions, he revealed that in his childhood, he made a pact that he'd never feel vulnerable to the economic hardship his family underwent. At a young age, too young, he carried the weight of adult concerns—heavy burdens that were impossible to resolve. Like many, he wasn't aware of how formative this childhood resolve would become in his life. Yet at eight years old, he'd determined its trajectory. This had much to do with his decision to go to college, the woman he married, and the career choices he made. Once decisions were made, the details lined up and he unconsciously put the tempo and direction of his life on automatic pilot.

In our discussions, John agreed the tempo he'd set was frantic and exhausting, yet the thought of remaking this childhood decision left him anxious. He was still running from the fear of poverty. Everyone knew he had placed enough in his bank account long ago to escape this possibility—everyone knew except John. He'd still be running if it weren't for that panic attack that got him a ride in an ambulance. That's when he began to ask, "What happened—where do I want to go?" Even more important, he realized that, emotionally, "I'm not eight years old any more."

Develop Alternate Paths

Once you're aware of some of your unrealistic expectations and unconscious, anxiety-driven choices you might have made to ward off fear, you now have a choice. You can take your life off automatic pilot. You can make choices by consciously deciding what's really important to you. After all, no one lives forever.

Ask yourself, "Do you want more time to spend with friends and family?" Laurie said yes. And John came to this realization when he lamented about his last raise. "All they're doing is giving me more money so I can buy more household help and fancier vacations. What they're not giving me is *time*."

Begin your own transformation by asking these questions. Do you need more purpose in your life than accumulating money? Is the stress and pressure you feel worth it? Do you have an alternate vision you want to pursue at a leisurely pace?

Do *not* feel you have to decide anything right away. This process could take a few years, especially if you need to wind down, unload, or finish previous obligations. Trust how formative just asking these questions will become. The right answers will eventually become clear. You will have already started to drift in the direction you want to go. But at this point, just have the courage to ask yourself these questions.

Begin by jealously guarding your time. You become a better steward of time by consistently attaching a value to the amount required for any endeavor you might take on *before you make the decision.* Check it against your long-range goals and updated destination. This is especially important if you have had a habit of automatically adding various good ideas to your agenda. But even though that idea may be terrific, if it isn't consistent with your long-range goals, let it go. Let me emphasize that. If a new idea doesn't align with your long-range goals, let it go.

Be careful of burdening yourself with mortgages and car payments that will hold you in bondage and reduce your choices. It's easy to be seduced by acquiring "stuff" to the point of making accumulation of money an end onto itself.

Live with a Purpose

Hundreds of years from now when everyone has enough material wealth, people will look back and recognize the struggle required to

> *We must each decide where to draw the line in our consumer-oriented society and ignore cultural messages that direct our lives.*
>
> *Hundreds of years from now when everyone has enough material wealth, people will look back and recognize the struggle required to switch from "materialism" to "purpose."*

switch from "materialism" to "purpose." Our present-day obsession with wealth will seem distant from the purposeful lives people of the future will live. They'll view our pursuit of material wealth with empathy and pity. They'll clearly define their existence on foundations of family, marriage, friendships, and community. Their workweek will be shorter and their vacation time will increase. The tempo and goals of our lives today will feel as remote to them as the lives of the cavemen who needed to hunt for what they ate.

I advise people to decide what to let go of and *simplify*. For example, one young man I worked with let go of potted plants because caring for them burdened his weekends when he really wanted more time for friends and sports. He'll likely resume his interest in gardening some day, but he, like many, easily gets caught up in caring for pets, homes, and investments, spending time on social duties, volunteering, and other undertakings that can be cut back for simplification.

Commit to People

Continually remind yourself that committing to your friends, family, and spouse is more important than accumulating wealth. This takes courage. You'll feel challenged because of current cultural values that dictate what car to drive, where to live, how to dress, and whom to socialize with. Don't underestimate the powerful images of "the good life" and their ability to put you back on automatic pilot. After you acquire financial security and a home, there's little to gain from accumulating money. Indeed, the more you acquire, the less money seems to help.

In my discussions with people who are new to having a great deal of money, their recurring question is, "Is this all there is?" After paying the price of their precious time, they conclude that having money isn't really all that great.

If the bin is brimming with grain and the animals are fed, it's time to pick up the palette and brushes and create a new vision. Paint a transcendent reality to live in—one that others can see and that's more rewarding than draping yourself in conspicuous consumption.

Create a vision that includes time to live.

Got Off the Road

I saw John periodically over three years. His course had indeed changed and he's no longer a wounded warrior. He got off the path to becoming CEO and viewed every promotion offer with discernment and skepticism. With every series of assignments he asked, "How would doing this affect all aspects of my life?"

Eventually, John resigned from the computer company, passing on offers for more money and any position he might want. He'd already decided to work for himself. He still works hard, but only for a few months at a time. During one of our last discussions, he explained his work as "putting together deals to develop, acquire, or take public different companies." In between deals, he enjoys large blocks of time to play and reflect. John even renewed a childhood love of freshwater fishing and visits a primitive lodge in Iowa on secluded fishing retreats.

The last time we talked, I asked John if he's ever afraid while alone in the woods at night. He misunderstood my question and told me he no longer runs from the monster that stalked him since childhood. I smiled with satisfaction and happiness for John. There was absolutely no need to clarify my question; he gave me the best answer possible.

Faith and doubt both are needed—
not as antagonists but working side by side—
to take us around the unknown curve.

LILLIAN SMITH (1897–1966), THE JOURNEY

4

When Dependency is Attractive

Jane couldn't stop thinking about the sandy-blond little boy who became separated from his mother as passengers were getting off the airplane at JFK airport in New York. The four-year-old came careening down the plane's aisle, frightened and crying.

"I lost my mommy," he screeched, running toward the flight attendant. His tears tumbled over his open mouth and his eyes searched frantically. Jane tossed her clipboard. It bounced off the chair's cushion as she caught the child in her outstretched arms.

"What's the matter... what's the matter? Are you lost?" she asked. He clutched her neck with one arm and got enough control of his panting terror to say, "I lost mommy... I lost mommy... mommy is gone."

"We'll find her," Jane reassured him. She smoothed the rippling waves of anxiety cascading through his back and shoulders, easing his shuddering body against her breasts.

A child's curiosity suddenly transformed into fearful separation in a world he couldn't yet handle alone. His distress vaulted to the surface.

He wouldn't let go of Jane, yet he still angled his head around to scan for his mother. Upon seeing her, he relaxed his clutching grasp. His mother gratefully took him from Jane's arms.

She profusely thanked the flight attendant, then helped her son let go of the panic he'd shown moments earlier. An hour later, as the flight resumed its trek to another city, Jane continued to feel a nagging worry for this boy, almost like an obsession.

A Lesson in Needing Someone

"Did you want to help that boy?" I asked Jane in her fourth month of therapy. I knew she wouldn't understand what I was getting at yet. Thirty-one years old and never married, she'd gone through four significant love relationships and uncountable others of less importance since her teenage years. She sought therapy for personal growth and relationship issues—specifically her reluctance to trust a partner who openly needed her.

"Yes," she said adamantly. She looked at me incredulously, wondering why I would ask her such a question.

"It wasn't a burden?" I went on, trying to punctuate for her that she *wanted* to be emotionally present for a stranger, albeit a little boy.

"No, of course not. I didn't question for a moment whether I was going to help him. I just did—he needed my help and I was there. Anyone would have done the same..." she insisted with some defensiveness but also with a conviction brought to the surface of her consciousness.

"He needed you."

"Yes."

"And he... it wasn't a burden."

"No... no, of course not."

Pause.

"Are you a burden when you need people?"

I asked the question softly, fully suspecting this was at the core of her struggle. A long silence followed. I watched her demeanor change from conviction to doubt. Beneath the surface, she struggled with the idea of someone actually wanting to be that emotionally caring about her. Her thoughts raced ahead to the even more frightening prospect of letting herself ever need *anyone* as much as the little boy needed her at that moment—a degree of need she rarely acknowledged to herself, never mind letting someone else see it. It was a need the sandy-blond-haired boy and one that she so willingly and lovingly met.

"Were you repulsed by the boy's crying?"

"No."

Her voice was muffled. She didn't look at me. She knew what I wanted her to reconsider.

She couldn't resurrect for herself the willing involvement she emphatically felt for the child. For the first time, she became anxiously aware of this defensive posture she assumed. She also became aware of a new possibility for herself—one without the safety afforded by vicarious participation. A possibility that meant reviving her archaic impressions regarding dependency. These unconscious impressions told her that no one would be there for her if her need was too great. Consequently, she'd learned to measure the need she showed other people.

This single defensive maneuver to bridle her need for dependency had shaped many aspects of her life and allowed her only vicarious

Pure vulnerability, although admittedly uncertain, brings out the most empathetic responses in other people.

participation in another's needs. It had a lot to do with choosing to be a flight attendant, attracting self-absorbed men, and creating diluted interpersonal connections that characterized all of her relationships.

Jane and I talked about why having an unadulterated pure need— as evidenced by the little boy she couldn't stop thinking about—was so attractive. Attractive in the sense that Jane wanted to be there for him. Clearly nothing else mattered but providing what he needed emotionally in that moment.

Pure dependency, as shown by the sandy-haired boy, can be very attractive. We need to express this level of dependency periodically throughout our lives and especially within marriage. We crave reassurance that someone would want to give us what we need simply because "they cared." Many fear others only give to them from a sense of obligation. Instead, we want that person to identify with our humanness and respond to how it feels to be in this world.

This capacity to feel compassion and empathy for others dwells within all of us. It's evoked by the expression of authentic and unadulterated need. Jane couldn't stop thinking about this boy because he ignited a long-held wish that she could need and receive as deeply as this boy had shown. Jane, however, couldn't accept this part of herself. She disdained the idea of her own dependency; her life seemed to mold itself around it.

To summarize, as a flight attendant Jane took care of others and was good at it. Her love relationships dissolved because of her difficulty bringing herself fully into them. Her preselection of self-absorbed men protected her from the vulnerability she secretly wished she could show. When she scooped up that little boy and hugged him, she was hugging the part of herself that had a deep, unsatisfied need for dependency. She couldn't stop obsessing about the welfare of this boy because she was dealing with her own feelings of dependency. The transcendent moment for Jane was this: She consciously accepted that she wanted to bring that quality into her life, allowing someone to be fully there for her.

Jane discovered that pure vulnerability is frequently attractive. There was nothing pretentious, controlling, or adulterated about the little boy's need... he was perfectly vulnerable. Pure vulnerability, although admittedly uncertain, brings out the most empathetic responses in other people. Although it felt risky for the boy, but precisely because he was so vulnerable, Jane didn't hesitate to be there for him. *Pure vulnerability is attractive.*

Jane finished her therapy after falling in love with a man she met on a trip to Bermuda. This relationship was different; she was able to give herself into it unlike her previous diminished investments. She found many small adult ways of "running down the aisle" and realized she needn't remain emotionally alone any longer.

Jane became mindful of when she held back feelings of doubt regarding career, friends, family and feelings of insecurity with her new love. Occasionally, she chose to reveal them in her soft tone, which I saw when she first told me the airline story. Jane can finally receive love and support because she looks as if she needs it at times. "It was always there for the taking," she mused, sighing with relief from the burden she'd imposed on herself.

The Attractiveness of Pure Dependency

Your assignment is to actualize the attractiveness of pure dependency in your own life and to allow others to love your humanness. The lesson calls for looking like you occasionally need something and allowing others to respond to your dependency. Use phrases like "I don't know, I'm not sure, I don't think I can go through that." Signal that you need something using passive and demur body language. You might be surprised and delighted that you, too, can tap into the caring capacity of others.

The mind is an iceberg;
it floats with only one-seventh of its bulk above water.

SIGMUND FREUD

(QUOTATION IN NEW YORK TIMES OBITUARY, SEPT. 24, 1939)

5

Road Rage and Aggression

Joe was blinded by the high beams from the 18-wheeler butting ominously close to the trunk of his compact car. The harsh light enveloped him and he couldn't avoid the glare off all three mirrors. He could hear snorting like it came from a charging bull—the intermittent sound of the downshifting diesel engine and the enormous brakes belching air as they ground against the drums to slow down. Joe had slowed down intentionally, his stubbornness evident. He was determined to cause the driver to change lanes and go around him. A few miles back, when Joe was trying to get onto the freeway, this semi driver had cut him off and didn't let him onto the freeway. Now it was Joe's turn to make the big bull slow down. Revenge was his.

This drama had shifted Joe's mood. The anticipation he'd been feeling as he headed into a three-day weekend got buried in his anger. In place of elation, he raged with feelings of revenge. So he'd maneuvered his car in front of this rolling behemoth, taunting its driver by forcing *him* to slow down. This normally rational and courteous man was playing a dangerous game in a compact car that afforded little protection. Yet he persisted driving in the number-four lane until his exit ramp approached, then stubbornly waited until the last moment to clear from the path of the 18-wheeled monster.

As Joe reached the bottom of the exit ramp, he ached from the tension in his neck and shoulders. He could hear his heart pound as it mobilized to meet the extreme perceived danger. Driving the streets in his neighborhood seemed tranquil compared to his surreal encounter just moments before. He took several deep breaths and stretched his cramping muscles, then muttered about his exasperation in getting involved at all. He could taste an unsavory concoction of embarrassment and relief. He knew he wasn't arriving home in the mood he had intended and wondered if his wife and children would read the dishevelment that churned inside.

The Wild West

In a 1998 study, the American Automobile Association (AAA)[1] found that aggressive driving has increased 51% over the previous five years. In 1997, the National Highway Traffic Safety Administration reported[2] that two thirds of all fatalities could be attributed to aggressive driving. NHTSA also reported that 64% of motorists say they frequently encounter other motorists who get unreasonably angry without real provocation. These studies show the anger on our roads is increasing, at times escalating into physical violence and gunplay, which are also on the increase.

Some of this aggressive behavior can be attributed to crowding on the nation's freeways and roads. In one decade, the number of cars on the road increased 11%, the number of miles driven increased 35%, while the number of new roads built has only increased 1%.[1] The reasons cited by the NHTSA survey include feeling rushed or behind schedule (23 percent); heavy traffic congestion (22 percent); careless/

inconsiderate drivers (12 percent); and complaints about immature/ young drivers (12 percent).[2] The toll of all this misplaced agression on our well being is enormous. In 1997, 41,000 Americans died in traffic accidents and an estimated two thirds of these involved aggressive driving.[2]

Why? Are people so frustrated that these angry feelings lurk just beneath the surface, waiting for an opportunity to be vented? If so, then why do they vent on the roadways? Why would people like Joe—normally courteous and gracious—get so aggressive?

Politeness Turned Aggressive

I'm struck by how we are more patient when encountering other people at the grocery store, for example. We wait our turn. We tell the clerk that someone else was next in line. We say thank you, please, and excuse me frequently.

But in a vehicle, there's a greater tendency to become petty, bold, insensitive, and aggressive. Why do unintegrated parts of ourselves surface when we're driving? What is it about the automobile that helps make it the right opportunity?

Perhaps it's the relative anonymity provided by the seclusion of tinted windows, sunglasses, and fleeting contact. We act with impunity because we can be down the road in a second; we remain unidentified. Unknown and unidentifiable people are objects of frustration that can be dismissed and disregarded. Like Joe, we react in ways that don't align with how we perceive ourselves and the person we show to others. Thus, the vast majority of people in our lives would never see this behavior.

Pressed for Time

Some might argue, "I'm not being aggressive. I'm pressed for time and always in a rush." Sounds reasonable, doesn't it? You can certainly become over committed with things to do and places to go. Don't fool yourself; you're rationalizing your actions. This is really about aggression and frustration, not about making time or being late. "No," you might say. "Sometimes a cigar is just a cigar—no deep hidden psychological meaning. I'm just late and I'm rushing." But have you ever done the math to know the difference in time saved if you traveled 75 miles an hour versus 65 miles an hour over a distance of, say, 15 miles? Look at this:

Speed and Time		
Speed	*Distance*	*Time to Get There*
65 mph	15 miles	13 minutes, 51 seconds
75 mph	15 miles	12 minutes
Time saved: 1 minute and 51 seconds on a 15-mile trip		

You save one minute and 51 seconds by rushing! Therefore, the aggressive driving that goes with being in a rush accomplishes little. Of course, if you encounter one red light after exiting the freeway and everyone you passed catches up, the actual time savings gets lost. But let's assume you are not encumbered by a red light, traffic congestion, road repairs, or accidents. The time savings of one minute and 51 seconds required you to drive fast, perhaps with one eye in the rear view mirror to spot a police officer ready to give you speeding ticket. Meanwhile your body tenses in a hyper-vigilant state and you arrive feeling more fatigued and less tolerant of stress-inducing events. You risk getting a speeding ticket, being forced to attend driving school,

In a vehicle, there's a greater tendency to become petty, bold, insensitive, and aggressive.

and/or paying more for insurance premiums, not to mention statistically increasing the odds of killing or harming yourself and others.

What It's Really About

One minute and 51 seconds isn't what this is really about. You can avoid a time crunch by leaving early and reaping the benefits that comes with it. (By the way, to really make up time and shave off five minutes on a 15-mile trip, you'd have to drive an average of *102 miles an hour!*)

It's really about unheeded feelings. Aggression, helplessness, and frustration—plus the need to feel like a winner. Unfortunately, these powerful feelings haven't been integrated into parts of life where they could do some good. In fact, they're trying to tell us something. If we heed their message, we can find something we apparently need that's worth having—much more than the pittance fought over on the freeways.

Unheeded, they frequently become expressed in our driving due to the anonymity mentioned. Our roads—populated with faceless entities, not people—become the flash points, the lightning rods, for passion associated with unfulfilled needs.

Expressing feelings of aggression can point out goals and dreams we have yet to realize. Some haven't ever dared to dream; others pursue their goals but have yet to reach them. Still others may have had success attaining their goals, but fail to absorb their aggression along the way. They're still prone to feel cheated. And when these feelings of being cheated are acute, they boil over into reactions such as road rage—reactions out of proportion to the offense.

These reactions represent an accumulation of the helplessness one inevitably experiences in life. Nothing is certain. None of us gets everything we want. Indeed, none of us knows exactly what we want. So our anger looks unconsciously for a target, a focal point.

We want to overcome feelings of helplessness by confronting them head on. It results in a cathartic explosion of accumulated anger without a worthwhile place to go.

Think again. You have plenty of places to invest your feelings so you can attain things more worthwhile than arriving 1 minute and 51 seconds earlier. Invest your feelings in your career, your social life, your family relations. Even grapple with your purpose in life, developing your spirituality and insight, understanding and relating to people better. These things don't come as readily as the false feeling of winning you get when you step on the accelerator.

Fish Worth Frying

Joe's encounter with the semi truck driver occurred shortly before he began therapy for personal growth. We uncovered his frustration with his failure to be promoted at work, especially after seeing others, often new arrivals, pass him by. Joe wanted more for himself but had overlooked facing his fear of failure when it came to taking risks. Through our discussions, he learned that the possibility of failure paled in comparison to the slow burn of frustration he felt watching others move beyond him. His frustration sought expression by confronting the mechanical bull on the road. His emotions were telling him he needed to change; the incident with the semi helped him recognize its urgency.

Today, Joe is a project manager in his company, a position he'd never been considered for because decision makers perceived he lacked assertiveness and avoided risk. Everything changed when Joe rediscovered those aspects of himself and learned to express them without taunting mechanical bulls.

Let Go of Road Rage

The lesson is to heed the message so theatrically displayed through road rage. The message says that you could be wasting important emotional resources on dangerous behaviors. Therefore, your assignment is to identify and practice letting go of these forms of expression. Instead, find answers and direction to more important questions in your life.

Also, delegate driving to a simple, non-emotional function that gets you from point A to point B. In your mind, minimize the advertisers' imagery of success, power, invincibility, sexual attraction, sophistication, and comfort. Don't let these images creep into your subconscious and become an overly significant part of your goals. Rather, accept that the ownership of a fancy car or driving aggressively will do little to help you attain what's really worth having.

---

[1] AAA Foundation for Traffic Safety, 1440 New York Avenue, N.W., Suite 201 Washington, D.C. 1998

[2] National Highway Traffic Safety Administration, 400 7th Street, S.W., Washington, D.C. 20590

Doctrine is nothing but the skin of truth set up and stuffed.

HENRY WARD BEECHER (1813–1887), LIFE THOUGHTS

6

The Evening News

The major network television stations placed reporters outside a home where a murder had taken place. The dark sky swirled with blue and red lights as a reporter snagged a police captain for information. The captain spoke into the reporter's microphone about a suspect, a victim, alleged connections, and probable motives as paramedics rolled a body bag past them and slid it into the waiting ambulance.

The next instant, viewers get taken back to the station's newsroom where a familiar, friendly broadcaster's voice announced "... and this is tonight's lead story. *This* is what's going on in your community."

It seems that journalism—whether it's on radio or television, in magazines or newspapers—is more sensational today than ever. You

> *Be conscious and vigilant about how you allow the news media to define your perceptions of the world.*

know how it works: ratings define newsworthiness, which accurately reflects audience consumption, which sells advertising.

Trusting Your Own Experiences

Murder and death are a prominent ingredient in this recipe. They touch on a subject in which we are all intimately interested—that we will die. It's a mystery, as Shakespeare once wrote, that involves "the undiscover'd country, from whose bourn, no traveller returns."

Death has long been a powerful focal point for many of the world's religious leaders, philosophers, and people like us. Thus it's also a powerful focal point for television station news directors who choose lead stories for their broadcasts. Television programming addresses the subject of death in short clips. It is delivered by warm, credible anchor people we grow to trust. As viewers, we're only a short distance from taking this all in as reality.

But does the nightly news *really* tell what's happening in our world? Does television accurately reflect the reality of our everyday lives? Or does it highlight the exceptional event, selected solely to capture our attention.

You can test this hypothesis for yourself by asking:

"Have I ever witnessed a murder?"

"Have I ever seen a dead body?"

"Have I ever seen someone get shot?"

"Have I ever seen a bullet wound?"

Rare is the person who actually witnesses a murder or gunshot wounds. Of course, exceptions include law enforcement officers and health care professionals. But for the vast majority of people, death and murder are rare occurrences in their lives. They go to work and school, build our families and friendships, obey the laws, drive reasonably, and don't settle our arguments with guns. Living normal lives isn't newsworthy; it won't sell advertising.

The World as You Know It

Newsworthiness seems to relate to negativity. When the news director of that station selected the murder above as the lead story, she excluded thousands of acts of generosity and dedication that had occurred that day. Objects invented, discoveries made, people helped, relationships built, beauty created, and love experienced. Thousands of quiet acts of heroism involve people who dedicate their efforts beyond their own self-interest. This is the stuff of our everyday lives, the fabric that's far more prevalent than crime. Although it holds our communities together, it won't sell advertising.

Nevertheless, reporting on quiet acts of heroism bring us closer to average experiences than murders do. Many journalists are disheartened by the content of the news they're trapped into disseminating, locked into the bind of economic realities and a devotion to market forces.

Don't Let Media Define Your World

Your assignment is to be conscious and vigilant about how you allow the news media to define your perceptions of the world. Many people live as if all strangers are bad (not simply unknown) and no one can be trusted. It's as if a child molester or abductor lurks behind every car door. Thankfully, all of these aberrations are rare exceptions.

During the build-up to the 2003 war with Iraq, I observed the effect television news had on several of my patients. CNN provided round-the-clock coverage, which significantly contributed to a process and feelings described as a *pervasive tension*. We were likely going to war and people could feel the tension during the weeks and months leading up to the conflict. Questions of whether Saddam Hussein had weapons of mass destruction that he might use could not be answered.

During that period, I noticed a distinct change among some of the patients in our group clinical practice, specifically an increase in the number of people with anxiety disorders. Panic attacks frightened those who'd had their first episode. Debilitating generalized anxiety and wearisome obsessive-compulsive conditions abounded. In every instance, these people were watching too much news coverage, so all of their treatment plans included turning off the TV.

Choosing a Focus

The same television broadcast that opened with a murder ended with a story about a driver who accidentally hit a deer sprinting across the freeway. The driver got out of his car and gave mouth-to-mouth resuscitation to the animal. In an instant, the deer sprang to its feet and resumed its sprint into the woods alongside the freeway. Then the familiar television anchorperson warmly smiled, thanked everyone for watching, and said good night as if all was right with the world.

Be careful how much you let the media shape your perception of reality. Trust what you know and rely on what you've experienced. Be skeptical of fast-food-like sources that rarely provide background information to help you understand the reality. There's danger in this world, but there's also far more good than media reports ever tell us. The story about resuscitating the deer says there's reason for hope and optimism—our society is making progress.

The folly of that impossible precept, 'Know Thyself';
till it be translated into this partially possible one,
'Know what thou canst work at.'

THOMAS CARLYLE (1795–1881)

1

Perfectionism and Procrastination

Jordan was in his chore-avoidance mode. Still the chores chided him for his attention each time he walked by the posted list. His wife's exasperation was simmering because of what she surmised to be Jordan's negligence and indifference. He sensed her frustration threatening to boil over at any moment in scalding expressions of anger. Yet he was moving as carefully as one could between the contradictory forces of approach and avoidance. He dreaded the thought of her assuming indifference or being unappreciative of efforts expended. Jordan cared very much for his wife. Her gung-ho style of heaping chores on the agenda, however, frightened him.

In our sessions, I learned something about perfectionism, procrastination, and the predicament Jordan had created. To him, undertaking home improvement projects felt like indentured servitude in which the debt expanded far more quickly than payments for that debt ever could. He only accepted doing these projects when his wife railed or when they loomed as absolute necessities.

In one of our early sessions, Jordan described the task he faced of changing the oil in his sport utility vehicle. He'd begun therapy because he realized how readily other people could accomplish these mundane domestic tasks, but he couldn't. He even agreed that some people, like his uncle, actually enjoyed the experience as they worked. This discrepancy in experience (they enjoyed it; he felt slavish)—along with his wife's threat of divorce—had prompted him to seek psychological consultation.

Jordan described a Sunday morning when he went into the garage and laid out what he needed to do an oil change. This task had become a necessity; his late model SUV had accumulated more than 10,000 miles since its last oil change.

He'd already lost two hours in minor distractions before he even started. He felt mild disappointment when he came across a new oil filter—if lost, it would have delivered him from having to begin this chore. Jordan rearranged the three-layer-thick newspapers several times before he finally got on his back and shimmied his way underneath the raised chassis. He used a crescent wrench to dislodge the oil plug and black liquid surged into the triangle tray 12 inches below. Jordan reached up to twist off the oil filter that had leaked oil down the engine's crankcase before he could completely unscrew it. A rag sopped up the slippery liquid and Jordan twisted on the new filter. Then he shifted his attention back to the oil oozing from the drain plug into the triangle pan, now a steady drip, drip, drip. He decided to let it drain a bit more when he noticed the accumulation of oil-crusted dirt on various parts of the underside of his vehicle. That's when his perfectionism kicked in.

Jordan began to wipe the parts clean. The more he looked for dirt, the more he saw and the scope of his chore grew by the moment. When one rag became heavily soiled, he crawled out from beneath the vehicle to get a roll of paper towels and a spray bottle of degreaser, then crawled back underneath. The oil was still dripping. He was now on automatic pilot and the destination he'd arrive at would be all too familiar.

Jordan first degreased the oil pan, assorted vacuum hoses and brake lines, as much of the engine's block as he could reach, the firewall, transmission housing, and more. Still he saw more cleaning to be done. Because of his complete absorption, he wasn't aware that two hours had passed since he first pulled the drain plug. The paper towel roll had become skinny and the mound of soiled towels increased. Finally the plastic spray bottle of degreaser emitted only air and Jordan was forced to retreat from beneath the vehicle. The oil still dripped and dripped and dripped, slowly but unrelentingly. Jordan's only thought was that he hadn't even begun to clean the engine compartment from above. He felt frustrated and the job still loomed incomplete. Once again, he'd arrived at that all-too-familiar place, exhausted and feeling worthless.

Tyranny of Perfectionism

Like any perfectionist, Jordan turned everything he did into a life-and-death struggle in the relentless way he approached it. He avoided doing chores because of the magnitude of the project he turned everything into. This project began as a simple oil and filter change but evolved into a hand-done, labor-intensive degreasing operation. Jordan hadn't consciously decided to do this. One thing led to another and, with little hope of preventing it, he got into yet another exhausting, futile experience. This was the work of his automatic emotional pilot he could neither control nor understand. It gnawed at him that he couldn't complete the job, which left him feeling inadequate on top of his exhaustion. Indeed, he faced this outcome each time he thought of beginning a chore. Not surprisingly, Jordan wouldn't change his oil again for a long time.

Addictive Behaviors

What sets people up for perfectionism that breeds procrastination? Why is perfectionism such an addictive behavior? People are not born perfectionists. Some model their anxious parents' example but others are self-made.

Being perfect becomes addictive to the perfectionist because it does feel good, however briefly, to accomplish something and do it well. Then perfectionism gets reinforced by the beneficiaries of a perfectionist's work because it's well done. However, people who suffer from the energy-robbing problems of perfectionism don't know how to effectively handle their anxiety, which renders them vulnerable to procrastination. They frequently leave large areas of their emotional life unresolved and free floating.

Free-Floating Anxiety

Life has risks. No matter what we do, we can't totally eliminate the reasonable risks we assume. Owning a car, falling in love, and purchasing a home all come with risks beyond our control. Changing jobs, moving, having children, even deciding on the color of new carpeting come with risks. Understandably, they become sources of anxiety. When we do not acknowledge these risks *and* accept the

People who suffer from the energy-robbing problems of perfectionism don't know how to effectively handle their anxiety.

They're susceptible to this behavior because they have difficulty accepting the ambiguity and doubt inherent in life itself.

possibility of the worst, they remain free-floating. Let me give you an example of acknowledgment and acceptance.

After my first child Adrienne reached the age of two and a half years, she began to run through the house with her hair flowing behind her. As I watched the swiftness with which she moved through space, I became conscious of every sharp edge, hard surface, and protruding corner. I winced at the disturbing images of physical harm and pain she could suffer if she violently encountered these surfaces. But I had a choice, even though no alternative was ideal.

As a parent, I could choose between allowing her to run carefree or trying to prevent injury by saying, "Be careful, slow down, you'll get hurt, that's dangerous, don't fall." If I chose the latter, I would have begun to define her world as a scary and dangerous place. I decided not to do this because I thought this damage would be more destructive than a physical injury. And doing so allowed her the reasonable risks of her behavior while acknowledging and accepting that physical harm was a possibility.

In making this choice, I had to accept emotionally that she would occasionally get hurt. On a broader scale, I had to accept my powerlessness to totally prevent accidents from happening anyway. I was left with the hope that any childhood injuries would prove minor, knowing there were no guarantees.

I had to accept this ambiguity about someone I cared for deeply. I had to acknowledge the possibility that her injuries could be serious. Even though the thought makes me feel ill and momentarily anxious. By acknowledging and accepting this possibility the fear doesn't float freely in my psyche. Of course, I've done what I reasonably could do to prevent injury. But over the years, I witnessed the occasional stubbed toe, scuffed knee, and swollen lip that distorted her delicate face. I know that life is frequently based on these kind of terms and it's heroic that we all carry on without ever fully being sure of anything.

Half-Empty Glass

Perfectionists have great difficulty living with life threads unsewn and feeling unable to control every outcome. The possibility for bad outcomes gnaw at them, making them feel incomplete and bare. The half-empty glass they see has no order and symmetry. They want assurance of an "absolute" when none is to be found. Insisting on a sure thing unconsciously becomes part of their lives when any task they undertake doesn't get completed until it reaches the lofty, unnecessary, and largely unattainable ideal of perfection. They're susceptible to this behavior because they have difficulty accepting the ambiguity and doubt inherent in life itself. They never make the tough emotional decisions, leaving themselves vulnerable to the vagaries of life.

Attach Words to Issues

Jordan's therapy was twofold. First, we began to attach words to a large number of issues. For example, he explained how he felt about being fired from work and about people criticizing him or not liking him. We discussed his feelings about taking risks and how badly failure would feel. In each instance, we looked at the worst-case scenario and the most likely outcome with an understanding that emotional acceptance of each possibility was necessary.

The second focus involved practicing "good enough." At first, "good enough" meant shoddy work to him and he recoiled in revulsion. He eventually accepted that anything more than good enough was draining his energy and ability to take risks—risks that were far more likely to produce returns than that extra margin of perfection ever would. One of Jordan's assignments involved practicing "good enough" in everyday decisions. It entailed defying his compulsion to practice perfectionism by driving his vehicle for an entire week without cleaning the windshield.

How Perfectionism Saps Energy

Your assignment is to recognize the energy-sapping ways that perfectionism creeps into the lives of high achievers—and into your life. Look at everything you do and ask if it's necessary or worth the additional time to complete. Listen to the message in your self-talk that might say, "I can relax when I get this done." Relaxation from exhaustion is different than choosing to relax when you still have energy available. If you find areas in which you are indeed more perfectionistic than warranted, ask yourself how you feel about this and what you haven't accepted about it.

You can also defy perfectionism wherever it manifests itself. For example, if you're excessively mindful of keeping your clothes neatly ordered, then intentionally allow a pile to build up on your bedroom chair. Your spouse may think this crazy, but you're indeed making progress in your personal growth. If you get carried away with cleaning in the kitchen, then leave the dishes sitting in the sink until the next day. Practice "good enough" in the chores you do and question tasks that perhaps shouldn't be on your agenda.

Today Jordan still isn't eager to take on chores at home—and he's not likely to enjoy doing them because he has too many negative feelings associated with household tasks. However, he does more of them and, consequently, has significantly reduced the number of times his wife gets angry at him. At work, he's able to take many more risks. The career advancements he's received reflect his increasing confidence. Jordan still smiles when he says "good enough" and avoids the lure of perfectionism that left him exhausted, doubtful, and forever procrastinating.

Be well, Jordan, and remember to not even *try* to be perfect.

People do not lack strength, they lack will.

VICTOR HUGO (1802–1885)

8

The Purgatory of Hope

Lisa knew she shouldn't go back into that house. Her mother had implored her not to talk with him—but to no avail. The sharp points of worry etched another line upon her face. Still, her bags were packed, waiting to return to the lodging she called home.

Lisa had taken up pleading his case, describing how he cried on the telephone and begged her to give him yet another chance. He'd reassured her that he could turn the page on their life and sketched out the things he would change. Yet her mother's loving concern ran too deep for her to wash her hands of the sordid mess in the way her father did years ago.

So Lisa found herself on the doorway's threshold about to re-enter the world she was all too familiar with—a world in which her sense of self would be smudged by his heavy-handed insecurities. There, the lines of reality sunk into a morass of subservience and feelings of inferiority that had become her life.

Her husband's contempt for Lisa was a daily balm liberally applied. It showed up as a dismissive sneer, which signaled an explosive verbal attack that threatened to plunge her into dark feelings of worthlessness. In their 12 years of marriage, Jason dominated her life and cooperated little. The few social outings they accepted usually resulted in embarrassment, knowing that others pitied the role she played. Many friends had long ago deserted her, unable to bear the pain that knowing Lisa entailed. Indeed, her persistence in continuing her relationship with Jason confounded everyone who ever cared about her. "I know—I know," Lisa has said without conviction countless times. She knew she'd keep returning to her abusive husband.

Last month, Jason's second affair was unearthed. Less than a week passed before he was demanding that Lisa just get over it. Her feelings of betrayal sickened her and contaminated her every waking thought. Lisa wondered what this woman had that she couldn't provide for her husband. The affair symbolized her failing report card as a wife and a person. So the night she returned, feeling tortured and utterly hopeless, she swallowed the entire bottle of her antidepressant medication. A trip to the emergency room to have the vile brew in her stomach extracted couldn't remove the pain that still throbbed in her gut.

Remaining Stuck

Lisa made hope and faith look like negative qualities. Her remaining friends felt either powerless to help her in her depression or were frustrated with what they viewed as her stupidity. Many abandoned her like her father had done.

For most of us, hope and faith are good things. They enable us to have the psychological courage to muster self discipline when we need to focus our behavior on a yet-unrealized goal. Hope bridges the doubts and insecurities involved in change, especially those entailed in pursuing dreams. This type of hope can mobilize a person. But Lisa's hope caused her to remain stuck and avoid making the changes necessary to improve her life.

Lisa lives in a realm I've named the Purgatory of Hope. It is about a manifestation of faith and perseverance gone wrong. From this place, any positive sign feeds the fantasy that things will improve. Whether or not these positive signs result in promised improvements has become unimportant; they simply serve to *sustain* hope. In Lisa's case, they frequently don't sustain hope and the abuse continues. Again, this is unimportant. The person trapped in the Purgatory of Hope has already received what she wanted—that is, reason to still have hope.

It appears that the Purgatory of Hope is used to avoid making changes. But that's not true. Hope in itself is the end product—a mental place in which just the thought of hope is familiar and sustaining. In this place, hope has become an optimistic emotion that's not dependent on anyone else. In this place, the promise for a better future provides positive feelings right now. It is limbo itself—a place that has become common and comfortable. Within it, someone like Lisa finds an unlikely set point that feels safe enough. She never really wants more.

Emotional Midway Point

The Purgatory of Hope is an emotional midway station between depression and contentment. It contains no emotional highs or lows and seems to contain few risks. That's why people who are stuck here stay. That is, they never feel the lows of disappointment nor do they fall from the lofty perch of losing something worth having.

In an effort to treat this problem, we attempt to move people like Lisa toward the depression that might change their life, because with

> *The Purgatory of Hope is an emotional midway station between depression and contentment.*

depression comes anger that just might mobilize them. But more often than not, inhabitants of this purgatory will not move.

Why would someone tolerate the deplorable situation people like Lisa volunteer to be part of? Because unhappiness has always defined their lives. If they acknowledge this, it means feeling the depression that they most deeply fear. They don't believe they can take on the depression and survive. This is why they prefer to "weather the arrows and stings of outrageous fortune" as a defense strategy. They likely adopted this storm-weathering strategy as children when they were powerless to change their situations.

Living Off Hope

People who live in the Purgatory of Hope usually have depressed or alcoholic parents. Unhappy marriages were routine and common. These children coped with the turmoil surrounding them by living off hope. Hope that things could improve. Hope inherent in positive fantasies. And hope unchallenged by reality.

Given the circumstances they were born into, hoping made sense. It was an act of courage no child should have to make. But as they grew older, denying reality made them oblivious to the early signs of bad situations and they continued to endure the pattern as if an albatross hung from their necks. As adults, they were no longer helpless and could learn to cope with their disappointments and depression. But they don't seem to know this; they continue to react to the chaos that surrounds them by ignoring reality and tapping into an endless reservoir of unwarranted hope.

At the other end of the continuum from depression, but equally feared, is contentment. The person stuck within the Purgatory of Hope also fears the rich emotional diet of contentment, made more potent when they add joy and happiness. They fear that they may grow to love this feeling, then face the unbearable risk of losing something worth having. This risk keeps them at the midpoint of hope.

So hope is a safer place than reality because it exists in their mind. They can resurrect it at will. They see all scenarios as possible, unimpeded by reality. It is theirs and theirs alone.

Hope That Holds You Back

Your assignment is to recognize the type of hope that holds you back versus hope that can assist you in moving forward. Hope that holds you back is often more subtle than the choices that challenged Lisa. It can appear in the form of maintaining a friendship that has become one sided. It could be a job that has drained your energy and spirit. It could mean making partner or career choices around an unconscious wish that a parent might love you. It could mean an extreme expectation that if you treat people fairly and with respect, they will reciprocate. These are fertile grounds on which the Purgatory of Hope might thrive.

Your assignment entails feeling the depression clamoring to be heard long enough to decipher any important message that it contains. The depression associated with a one-sided friendship could mean it's time to confront the person and/or leave the relationship. It could mean reconsidering your goals and reexamining what you want to achieve. It could mean accepting that people are not always fair, competent, or perfect without becoming cynical or distant.

Remember that ideals can rarely be implemented but they're still important beacons of growth. Never allow hope to shackle you.

Lisa never left Jason through the two years I knew her. Similar to her friends and family, I wince when I think about the life she has chosen knowing it could be very much different. It was difficult to work with Lisa knowing that her history and experience suggested she would continue to go back to Jason no matter what I counseled and no matter how hard I attempted to raise her depression. Six months after her therapy ended, I heard from a physician that Lisa was treated in the emergency room. A year and a half later, I heard that she was living in Laura's House, a local shelter for women.

It doesn't have to be this way, Lisa. You can have so much more.

If you do not tell the truth about yourself
you cannot tell it about other people.

VIRGINIA WOOLF (1882–1941), THE MOMENT AND OTHER ESSAYS

9

Self-Criticism

This was Ashley's sixth session in individual therapy. She just corrected herself twice in mid-stream while completing her thought. It was as if someone next to her examined her every word for honesty and accuracy, waiting to pounce on her for the tiniest distortion or mistake. She couldn't complete any thoughts or feel free to speculate, for this invisible overlord demanded precision. It was never satisfied no matter how hard she tried. It burdened her with a fatigue that ached in her halting, quivering voice. My reassuring words did nothing to relieve the onslaught she imposed on her personhood every moment of her existence. And when I tried to gently point out this relentless internal deliberation, she only felt criticized. The criticism further stoked the searing flames of self-recrimination at a paralyzing pace. I wanted to grab the tortured little girl inside and shield her from this demon. Yet I knew Ashley had to find her own way to contentment and self-acceptance.

Self-Talk Defines Us

We all engage in self-talk, which is a defining aspect of being human. This self-talk, or cognitions, can take the form of a warm fantasy, a replay of previous events, even anticipation or planning. In Ashley's case, it takes the form of self-criticism.

As with everything, too much or too little self-talk can be a bad thing. Ashley clearly experienced too much self-talk, especially the self-critical type. Engaging in too much fantasy self-talk puts a person in danger of living life as a vicarious experience rather than a genuine one. Similarly, too much self-talk about previous events leads to obsessive rumination. Finally, too much self-talk centered around anticipation and planning contributes to feelings of anxiety that stem from trying to gain more control than is possible.

At the other extreme, too little self-talk involving fantasy can rob a person of dreams and possibilities not yet explored, tethering them to the ordinary. Too little self-talk around events suggest an ego that rarely observes and thus fails to learn from experience. Too little anticipation is the province of those who habitually avoid responsibility. In these cognitive styles are hidden themes that are defended and concealed from the person's awareness.

Healthy Self-Criticism

Everyone needs an optimal amount of self-criticism. At its best, it functions as a gentle discipline that provides clarity and insight. When it's a harsh critique, distortions abound and perspective gets lost. A gentle discipline fulfills the purpose of self-criticism, which is to help people profit from their experiences. Those with too little self-criticism continually repeat the same mistakes in life and their folly eventually becomes apparent to everyone around them. Those with too much self-talk (like Ashley) live a tortured life with little contentment or joy.

Here's what the right amount of critical self-talk sounds like after you make a mistake: *"I did do that. (Sigh) Oh well, I won't do that again."*

Your assignment is to practice this gentle form of self-talk after making a mistake. Anything more drains self-esteem that's needed for taking worthwhile risks; anything less destines one to repeat the lesson that an emotionally corrective experience offers. So the goal in controlling your self-talk is to train yourself to learn from mistakes while refusing to engage in unnecessary condemnation. If you get it, you get it, and that's enough. If it isn't enough, then you've internalized a despotic expectation for yourself that you don't need.

Mistakes are part of a healthy life. In fact, if you're not making mistakes, then you're probably not experimenting enough with life or reaching far enough with your dreams. Somewhere in your life, move beyond the safe and conservative (after doing your due diligence, of course). Athletes practice this by adopting a phrase that says, "Go for it." You can make room in your repertoire by saying something like, "Win some; lose some."

Not Expecting Perfection

Ashley was eventually able to lessen her harsh internal dialogue by accepting that she couldn't and shouldn't try to be perfect. She took comfort in the fact that the majority of people lead successful lives without needing to be extremely careful. Ashley finally relaxed and allowed her expressions to become unbridled and resolute.

More deeply, Ashley (and also John, who had a panic attack in "Wounded Warriors") had been motivated by fear rather than simple pleasure. People like them want to prove they're not failures. Indeed, they believe the best anyone can do is avoid failure. This belief leads to a meager existence without joy. It never leads to success.

An optimal amount of self-criticism
functions as a gentle discipline that
provides clarity and insight.

The majority of people are motivated by success, drawing confidence and satisfaction from their accomplishments. This progresses into the ability to take risks, to dream, to adopt a spontaneous interpersonal style, to make necessary changes as life moves on, and more. Certainly this style is far less draining energetically than Ashley's style.

How Self-Criticism Works in Your Life

Your assignment is to monitor how self-criticism works in your life. Ask whether your self-talk is either too harsh or non-existent, then observe how and when it appears during the day. If you find your self-criticism isn't moderate, then find a psychologist to help you alter your style.

A weed is a plant whose virtues have not yet been discovered.

RALPH WALDO EMERSON (1803–1882)

10

 conco

Getting Older

Vicki loathed getting injections or having blood drawn. She found them to be more uncomfortable than most people did. However, her desire to eliminate the mild but visible cellulite deposits in her thighs was apparently much stronger than her reluctance to be injected.

When she went for her liposuction treatment, she winced as the IV for general anesthesia was inserted into her arm. She looked away as the nurse anesthetist established the line on her first attempt. Vicki's motionless body belied the tenseness she felt as she lay on the gurney. Her brown hair was encased in a turquoise-colored cap not unlike those worn by someone in food service. Her legs were marked with a grease pencil that highlighted the unacceptable fat deposits she couldn't make disappear no matter how much she dieted or exercised. Her heart began to race when they switched on the giant clam-shaped light as her physician entered the operating room. The nurse anesthetist told her to count backwards from 99. In her final moment of consciousness, she was staring at a large jar and a table laden with instruments.

Letting Go of Youth

Women are especially vulnerable to pressures of maintaining the look of youthfulness. These pressures can be measured by the explosive increase in the number of liposuction, tummy tucks, face-lifts, cheek-nose-jaw reconstructions, breast augmentation, facial resurfacing, and other aesthetic surgical procedures that are being performed. Men have also participated in this quest for perpetual youth, requesting some of these procedures as well as hair transplantation and penile enlargement. The latter in particular seems to be an attempt to fulfill a psychological need beyond youthfulness—perhaps to bolster their self-esteem.

Less intrusive attempts to pursue youthfulness involve the multi-billion dollar cosmetic industry. Body and facial preparations, hair products, and make-up offer benefits that can't be substantiated by science. Excessive exercise (beyond what's required for health) can also be seen as the pursuit of preserving youthfulness.

This overemphasis on looking young centers around our feelings about aging, which tend to be negative. We see these negative feelings manifested in how we dress, look, and behave. One of my patients echoed this sentiment with this joke:

QUESTION: "Do you know what the 'F' words are?"
ANSWER: "Forty and fifty."

The Downside of Aging

I wouldn't be honest if I didn't admit that aging entails some negatives. It does. Aging includes persistent aches and pains, decreases in physical energy, and catastrophic breakdowns in certain body parts.

> *You continue to age... and any diminished ability to accept that fact will prove far more painful than cosmetic surgery.*

These are not things to rejoice about, but all of life's stages entail negative experiences.

Do you remember the emotional swings of childhood when frustrations proved so overwhelming, we'd dissolve into tears and anger? How about the awkwardness of adolescence when we were expected to behave like adults despite the sea of inferiority that surrounded us? Or how about the ever-present anxiety of financial solvency that begins in young adulthood? Every stage in life has its positives and negatives.

Aging ends in death, one might argue. True enough. However, death handled well can be a surprisingly positive experience. For example, having hospice assist at a person's impending death can help everyone involved prepare for the clinical, spiritual, and relational aspects of dying. Hospice frequently helps families and friends finish old business, express wishes for loved ones, and say goodbye. Those facing death say it isn't nearly as bad as they anticipated; those who handle death well actually welcome it.

In my seminars, I ask this question that gets to the core of the aging issue:

"Is wisdom a fair trade for youth?" I poll the attendees on their opinions and, on average, get the following response:

Yes	*No*	*Don't Know*
10%	20%	70%

The percentage of people who answer "yes" rises with the increasing age of the attendees. But it never goes beyond 25%!

Wisdom

I think wisdom *is* a fair trade for youth, especially since it's the only choice we have. If we don't consciously accept our aging selves, then we're vulnerable to pursuing—at great emotional and financial costs—the illusion of perpetual youth. The financial costs are the more visible of the two. It's easy to waste resources on cosmetics that don't deliver on their promises or undergo surgical procedures that cannot buy a single extra minute of life. You might say, "But I look better because of them. If it makes me happy, what's the harm?"

The emotional cost lies with the time and resources you spend traveling down a false path. In truth, larger breasts or a larger penis, decreases in fat or increases in hair, never substantially alter one's experience of the world. People experience satisfaction at first. But in time, those feelings dissolve and their usual emotions remain. Down the road, they ultimately conclude that these interventions really didn't matter.

Some of you may have already had or are contemplating cosmetic surgery. If this is so, I am not suggesting it means the end of any chance you'll have for emotional well being. Try not to go overboard by pursuing physical alterations. Permanent eyeliner, lasik surgery, and skin peels seem the most benign. And having breasts implants and liposuction along with good nutrition and more exercise isn't all that bad. Facial and penis reconstruction are too much. You are good enough being just who you are.

Wishing for Improvements

Don't underestimate the power of your fantasies for "improvements" in your body image and their ties to the ageless human wish for immortality. Aesthetic improvements are only skin deep. Realize that any improvement in facial features won't result in sustained feelings of happiness. In the next chapter titled "Contentment versus Happiness," we'll discuss how happiness is not a place where one lives but an emotional place we only visit. Contentment, however, is a place to spend the majority of our emotional time. By definition, people are *not* content (or accepting) of their faces (or themselves) if they allow a physician to rearrange the faces' natural evolution with a scalpel. Indeed, this is an act of *discontentment* in pursuit of an illusion. That illusion is eternal youth, pursued in lieu of self-acceptance. It spurs and mocks the crucial practice of contentment.

"I like these physical changes. What's the harm in them?" you may ask. I'd answer that by saying any actual happiness experienced will be temporary. To go down this path is to wrestle with a goal you can never attain—recapturing your youth.

No one has been able to reverse the biological clock; any overt changes will only invite comparisons to faces and bodies currently living in that period of life. Disappointment is subtle but inevitable. *Time rolls onward and you continue to age, and your diminished ability to accept that fact will prove far more painful than cosmetic surgery.*

Feeling Secure Diminishes Need

Vicki did not have any further cosmetic surgery once the liposuction was complete. She was quite pleased with the results. A month after the surgery, she came to her appointment wearing tight jeans that she said she would have previously never had worn. She said they used to make her look fat. She occasionally thinks about breast augmentation and silicone injections for her lips, but hasn't had it done.

Soon after her liposuction, Vicki met a guy named Allen in night school where she was studying graphic design. Thanks to her hard work on herself, this relationship resulted in a good marriage. About two years after her wedding, we discussed whether she was considering having more surgery. She quickly dismissed the idea and spoke about her desire to have a baby and restructure her career. I believe that her feeling secure in her marriage to Allen diminished her need to have cosmetic surgery.

Your assignment is to temper your pursuit for body image improvements to what's needed for your health, longevity, and pleasure. Don't underestimate how vulnerable you might be to fantasies of unending youthfulness. Rather, seek wisdom as a fair trade for youth and accept your aging body. That's where you'll find contentment.

All truth passes through three stages:
First it is ridiculed;
Second, it is violently opposed; and
Third, it is accepted as self-evident.

ARTHUR SCHOPENHAUER (1788–1860)

11

Contentment versus Happiness

Happiness is not a place where we can live continuously. Nevertheless, this notion that happiness, like love, is supposed to be a constant experience has been embedded in our expectations. Using these phrases reveals a collective ideal most people harbor:

"I want to be happy."

"I'm happily married."

"I'm happy with my work."

"He makes me happy."

"I'm happy to be home."

"I won't be happy with this pair of shoes."

"I'd be so happy if I could afford a car like that."

It all suggests a constant emotional state when, in fact, happiness is never a constant for anyone. Think of the times in your daily experience when it's not happiness you experience but worry, depression, overwhelm, boredom, excitement, and so on. Although we experience a range of feelings, we can't feel nearly as much happiness (or as much love) as proclaimed by the norms of our culture.

This unrealistic expectation for happiness reflects that, on some level, we want to believe happiness is much more possible than it is. We cling to this by believing the conquest of one more goal or the accumulation of one more thing will make us happy. Consequently, many of our paths are heavily influenced by this unattainable expectation. The goals we select, the activities we pursue, can reflect our unconscious hope for perpetual bliss.

The Promise of Happiness

When you look at a new car or a beautiful house—nicer than what you have—does it promise you more happiness? Do you momentarily envision a life filled with more joy than you already have? Have you subtly but conclusively made up your mind this change will lead to more positive feelings about yourself and your life?

Unaware that we organize our lives around these subtle but powerful influences, we follow the pursuit of "stuff." The inevitable result is feeling discontent and empty. When we acknowledge that, we pick ourselves up, brush off the disappointment, and look for the next "fix" by acquiring one more thing or accomplishing one more goal.

At times, this need for a "fix" can take the form of substance addiction. Early on, our craving for happiness is temporarily satisfied with feelings of euphoria through the use of drugs and/or alcohol. So we get seduced into believing we can control our supply of happiness with continued usage.

I'm suggesting that the ravenous hunger for happiness must not be allowed to extinguish moments of contentment. We can learn to recognize these moments. With recognition comes the chance to draw emotional supplies that sustain us. This lesson and awareness often goes unlearned until one confronts a life-threatening illness. At this critical juncture, we see perspective and balance and wonder what we worried about before receiving this perspective-altering news. In Chapter 2, for example, Laurie's experience with breast cancer forced her to reconcile what was important to her and learn to live in the moment.

Where No One Will Ever Live

Advertising—on television, in glossy magazines, through showroom windows, and so on—shows places where no one actually lives. Rather, it's an effective tool to manipulate an insidious wish for endless and controllable happiness. For example, a recent beer commercial depicted a group of 20-something adults playing touch football on the beach. They seemed like such a close group of friends. Everyone was outgoing, playful, athletic—all the women beautiful and all the men handsome. Everyone in the group appeared to be cloaked in a cocoon of support, friendship, and opportunities to play with many fun people. Their lives seemed intertwined in things that matter. Perched amid this cornucopia of perfection was the beer, which linked them together. Drinking this kind of beer was an important resource for achieving the abundant, controllable happiness depicted in the ad. The larger meaning implied that this utopia was indeed available.

The power of pairing basic needs with a product such as beer shouldn't be underestimated. How many social events have you attended in which alcohol wasn't served? Very few. My point doesn't center on the wickedness of alcohol; it's about what we do, buy, or ingest to reach for that continuous state of happiness—a state no one ever achieves. A feeling no one has ever sustained. An illusion enshrined in our psyches. It beckons us but forever remains beyond our grasp. It's like the model home displaying an open book on the

The ravenous hunger for happiness must not be allowed to extinguish moments of contentment.

coffee table, flawless fruit in a bowl on the counter, bathrooms without toiletries, and children's bedrooms without clutter. It's a place where no one lives.

If Not Happiness, Then What?

You can never be happy all of the time or even most of the time, but you can feel contentment most of the time if you try. Contentment doesn't sweep through you like the eruption of excitement or surprise. It's subtle, like when the weather turns warm and you make it part of the moment you're in.

We find contentment by appreciating all the small positive things. We practice the art of realizing these small things on a day-to-day basis. We acknowledge our partner's contribution to making our house a home. We look for the many positive attributes about the people in our lives rather than focusing upon their shortcomings. We fully immerse ourselves in a moment of levity, in a moment of warmth, in a moment of connection. We find contentment when we choose to see it.

Practice Contentment Wherever You Are

Your assignment is to *practice contentment* wherever you are, rather than *pursing happiness*. Practice contentment while sitting in a traffic jam by letting go of time urgency and becoming absorbed in the radio. Practice contentment in your work by letting go of stressors and focusing only upon the task at hand. Enjoy the simple satisfaction of completing each project.

Practice contentment by focusing on those around you—your family and friends—and on the beauty near you. Slow down to smell the flowers, feel the sun, be lifted by the breeze and empowered by the sweeping vista. Contentment surrounds us always. It's available for the taking if we pursue this fairest of all maidens.

The future is only a series of nows.

NICHOLAS EVANS, 1995

12

Finding Peace

The front yard was still covered in foot-high snow although the thermometer's arrow pointed just shy of 40 degrees. Ben squinted to look at the brilliantly illuminated landscape corralling his house. He stood, bare-chested and holding his head erect. He was baptized by the sunlight and the invisible warmth shimmering from the masonry and wood dental alcove of the formal entryway outside his home. Breezes carrying a crystallized coldness didn't permeate the pocket of warmth. The protective orb of radiated heat invited Ben to remain focused within. Feeling content, he eased down the wall shrouded in the sun's veiled presence. As his eyes adjusted to the sunlight, he fixed his gaze on the serenity of the outdoor scene before him, completely absorbed in the moment.

Ben could hear the cry of a hawk mixed with the sound of the wind, purified and given voice by the evergreen trees that touched its passage. The scope of his awareness increased as he heard the hum of an unseen airplane in the distance. Every sound became louder while the surrounding land and sky carried on its ageless trek.

In the stillness of the morning, Ben thought about nothing but seemed aware of everything. He surrendered any sense of purposefulness to the ancient procession he was now simply a part of. He hadn't noticed the present or felt it quite this way before. The sudden intrusion of a telephone's ring caused the moment to melt away with the snow that trickled from the window ledge.

A Natural High

Ben had been absorbed in the present moment until the telephone rang. His concentration was so focused, he found this atypical experience intoxicating and pleasurable.

We often labor under the persistent noise of uncontrolled thoughts and the debilitating feelings these thoughts engender. Runaway thoughts dominate our experience and we struggle for control to stay focused. Strong feelings associated with a meaningful event or person can cause us to shift our thoughts from the present to the past.

To cope with this lack of focus, many people ironically turn to distractions that interfere even more. In effect, they take in more but different noise. Distractions range from the benign effect of watching television to the drastic assist of taking drugs. Their attention is filled with excessive thoughts about the future and/or the past, diminishing their ability to live in the present. One can hear their thoughts go back and forth, to the past and to the present in a relentless, punishing torrent of noise.

How often do we hear people talk about "going home and relaxing with a beer" as a way to shift their moods. At its best, this ability to shift is a skill and an important component of emotional intelligence. At its worst, it accounts for our vulnerability to the use of psychoactive substances like alcohol and drugs.

This chapter is about building a specific skill into your daily existence—the psychological discipline to remain in the present. This practice alone can profoundly affect every aspect of your life. It's illustrated by a concept called The Time Line.

The Time Line

The Time Line shown here illustrates just where, in time, our thoughts focus. That is, are they predominantly in the present? Are they ruminating about the past? Or are they overly anticipating the future? It's useful to be aware of where your thoughts tend to focus. If thoughts predominate in either the past or future, dysfunction can result.

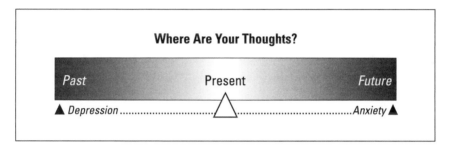

Where Are Your Thoughts?

Past　　　　　Present　　　　　*Future*

▲ Depression ..../\\....................................Anxiety ▲

Where along the time line is the predominant focus of your thoughts? How much can you remain in the present? How much time do you spend thinking about the past or the future?

The Future

Some people spend too much time obsessing about the future. You can hear this fixation, for example, in worries about an important date, the well being of loved ones, concerns around achieving goals and acquiring money, possibilities of rejection, and even death.

These thoughts are all based in the future and reflect the cognitive practice of anxious anticipation. But after they've prompted reasonable preparation and planning, future-oriented obsessions serve no useful purpose. Consequently, they are exhausting and can lead to a chronic state of worry that's difficult for others to tolerate. They waste emotional energy and lead to missed opportunities, even anxiety. We are likely to avoid change, reject worthwhile risks, and experience more stress and deterioration in our physical health.[1] Once we look into the future to check our direction and prepare for a specific goal, we need to let go, experience life, and pursue goals in the present. This breaks down life's goals into manageable tasks accomplished in the present. Those who have developed their ability to be fully absorbed have called this state as being in "the flow."

The Past

Some people spend too much time obsessing about their past. You can hear their ruminations in their expressions of guilt, regret, missed opportunities, and doubts about what could have been. Their extreme concern about previous events is usually accompanied by self-recriminations.

Of course, it's useful to reflect on past behaviors, experiences, and feelings, but only to a point. In doing so, we can learn from our life lessons. Those who reflect too little about the past fail to learn from their experiences and often find themselves repeating the same experiences and mistakes. Those who reflect too much about the past are often too critical of themselves.

Once we've looked behind us and recognized lessons learned, it's time to let thoughts of the past go through practicing a gentle self-discipline. Releasing them helps preserve energy to fully commit to the present. People who cannot do this often suffer from depression. They're likely to realize fewer goals, derive less from the present, and suffer deterioration of their physical health.[2]

---

[1] Sheldon Cohen, a psychologist at Carnegie-Mellon University. Cohen worked with scientists at a specialized colds research unit in Sheffield, England. They carefully assessed how much stress people were feeling in their lives, and then systematically exposed them to a cold virus. Among those with little stress, 27% came down with a cold. Among those with the most stressful lives, 47% got the cold—direct evidence that stress itself weakens the immune system. c.f. Goleman, Daniel *Emotional Intelligence*, 1995

[2] In this study, 2,832 middle-aged men and women were tracked for 12 years. They felt a sense of nagging despair and hopelessness and had a heightened rate of death from heart disease. And for the 3% or so who were most severely depressed, the death rate from heart disease, compared to the rate for those with no feelings of depression, was four times greater. c.f. Goleman, Daniel *Emotional Intelligence*, 1995.

People suffering from an agitated depression often rely on distraction or sleep. When they verbalize their thoughts, they're painful to be around. They have a tendency to flood those in their presence with emotion. These are undisciplined minds despite a frequently stringent, overt appearance of self-examination and an uncompromising standard. They have little control over their thoughts. The temporal dimensions of past, present, and future are expressed almost at once. Their cognitions are like a blasting radio that has no volume control. In time, it exhausts their energy; they know no peace and rarely experience contentment.

When I listen to some people recount their life stories in psychotherapy, I hear their thoughts jump ceaselessly between the past and future. Back and forth they jerk their emotional lives between these temporal emotional poles. It's like throwing an automobile's transmission between drive and reverse while pressing on the accelerator. This poor cognitive discipline is extremely painful and always unfruitful. Its consequence is agitated depression.

The Present

Right now is the present. Right now, at this moment, as you read this chapter, your attention should not be focused any other place. But are you fully absorbed?

You know where you have to be an hour from now, tomorrow, and in several months. But right now you are in the present, focusing upon these words, blocking out thoughts that poke into the future and dally in the past. So pay attention. Only in the now are all things possible.

The hallmark of the present is the ability to stay absorbed. If you cannot focus, these words mean little. When you give reign to these intrusive thoughts, you're no longer in the present and words on paper won't mean anything to you. You may be subverting your decision to read by extraneous noise and other undisciplined thoughts. Some are distracted in practically everything they do as if they're in multiple places at one time. Not only is this exhausting, but it diminishes the experience of the moment.

We dilute the value of many experiences by not being in the present. This forfeiture of experience diminishes the quality of everything we do. In his book *Wherever You Go There You Are*, Jon Kabat-Zinn stresses the need to remain mindful of the present. In *Thoughts Without A Thinker*, Mark Epstein shows how the professional mental health community can help patients find other ways of being and perceiving this world. Ultimately, it helps them find peace.

In the example earlier, Ben's alternative way of being in "the flow" was triggered by sensory input—the bright sun and warm alcove amidst the coldness and nature's beauty. By paying attention to his senses, he was able to override his thoughts. His experience standing in the alcove was about being in the present for the first time in a long time. He realized a surrender of the purposeful way he experiences the present to find full absorption of what that moment contained. Captured by the rhythm of nature, which is always there for the taking, he tapped into a strong level of focus and let go of his purposeful behaviors. He became aware of things he ordinarily would not have realized. He felt the ready availability of contentment. He was at peace.

Until this experience and our subsequent discussions, Ben was rarely riveted to the present or mindful of his experiences. Like many, he viewed all passage of time as purposeful, goal directed, and frequently outside of the present. Since then, he's resolved to practice staying in the present.

Become Mindful of the Now

You can develop the discipline to stay in the present by becoming mindful of when your thoughts detach you from the now. When this happens, your assignment is to begin to pull yourself back. If extraneous thoughts persist, make a conscious decision to stop whatever you are trying to

> *You have a greater ability to control your*
> *emotional reactions to events than*
> *controlling the events that will happen*
> *throughout your life.*

do, and explore what they have to say. By practicing this, your ability to stay in the present will be strengthened and your experiences enhanced.

The lesson is to practice absorption in the moment. The goal is to acquire the discipline to avoid distraction while creating an emotional tone of quiet acceptance. Accept the fact that you have a greater ability to control your emotional reactions to events than controlling the events that will happen throughout your life.

Let me say that again. We can decide how we will react to the events in our lives, even though we can't determine what will happen to us. Accepting this fact helps us use emotional discipline to remain in the present.

Think of the small but countless ways to implement this in your life. When you're talking with someone, refuse to become distracted, break eye contact, or allow a sense of time urgency to intrude on the moments you're sharing. While driving, refrain from allowing the press of lateness, traffic congestion, or ambition to impinge on your ability to feel content in the now. When at work, create an emotional orb in which you're fully present. Strive to avoid getting caught up in the stressors and reactions of other people. If something pulls you out of the emotional tone you have assumed, get back into it. Stay mindful of it. Adopt a tone that's peaceful, content, and present-focused.

Practice this emotional tone wherever you are and no matter what is happening. It will not come easy. However, in time, this skill becomes stronger and your ability to maintain an emotional equilibrium will improve.

Practice contentment and live life in the only time frame possible—the present.

Part 3: About Love and Marriage

A 16th century Bishop once said...
Marriage has less beauty but has more safety than the single life.
It's full of sorrows and full of joys.
It lies under more burdens but it is supported
by all the strengths of love
and these burdens are delightful.
In the end, all you can do is commit to the people you love,
hope for some good luck and good weather.

FORCES OF NATURE, *1999*

13

Romantic Ideals that Hurt:
The Bridges of Madison County

For those who haven't read the book or seen the movie The Bridges of Madison County, here's a brief overview.

The story is actually told as a flashback through the eyes of Francesca's children as they sort through her belongings after their mother's death. It takes place on a small Midwest farm in the late '50s. Francesca, an Italian-born woman and now middle-aged, had met her husband in Italy while he was a soldier and they settled in Iowa's Madison County.

It opens as Francesca's teenage daughter and son leave to go out of town for four days with their father. Shortly after their departure, Francesca meets Robert Kinkaid, a photographer on assignment for *National Geographic* to take pictures of covered bridges in Madison County. Despite her attempts to avoid getting involved with him, she falls in love, which awakens a passion and excitement that she (and all of us) long for. The day after her family returns home, she's in a pickup truck following Robert Kinkaid's truck to the edge of town, watching him drive away and out of her life permanently. With feelings of enormous conflict, she chokes back the tears. The rain falls.

Prior to their tearful farewell, Francesca seems to know that going with Kinkaid would permanently alter their short but intense relationship. Their four magical days of passion would dissolve into a more complicated reality with each passing mile. The collision between his nomadic life style and her obedience to obligation would await them around the first bend in the road. Lo and behold, their feelings for each other would also include the familiar mix of contentment and ambivalence—a mix of feelings we were familiar with as we left the theater, tissues in hand. Like Francesca, we were soaked in sadness for an unrequited love—one that "comes along only once in a lifetime." Nevertheless, I found myself wishing she had lifted that truck's door handle a little farther, swung to his side, and chose passion over duty (though it likely would have proven to be no better than staying).

Heartfelt Loss

Since the release of this movie, I've heard many honest but painful admissions from many women in my consultation room. Their admissions reveal a heartfelt loss of a romantic ideal we've not come to terms with in our western culture. Each trouble-laden comment was essentially a variation of, "My husband is no Robert Kinkaid."

The movie's disturbing encounter with the emotional reality of marriage has rekindled a question I've long pondered. That is, *what is it about us that longs for a love more perfect than the one we have?*

This desire for a perfect love is in no way the exclusive domain of women. In its most tragic form, it shows up when an older man abandons his marriage and family for the mythic younger woman. In its less drastic forms, we replay private fantasies of a perfect love, vicariously enjoyed by images of an attractive, wealthy person or a sensual, evocative movie.

Each time, however, there is a subtle but ever-present price to pay. We're aware that somehow we, in our apparently mundane circumstances, aren't worthy of so much happiness and pleasure. Every insincere advertisement with a pretty face, every romantic story with its contrived outcome, extracts its price. Romance books and concepts like "soul mates" pander to this unattainable wish by pushing the ideal beyond what's actually occurring. Nevertheless, we seek this vicarious participation in a perfect love even though it sets us up for disappointment. On and on, we're haunted by comparing the ideal of "what could be" with the reality of "what is."

Expectation of Perfect Love

This ideal inevitably vanishes into the oceans of time and reality. The beaches I've gone to are dotted with, might I say, ordinary people. I remember a vague sense of disappointment when I first traveled to Hawaii, a land I envisioned as absolute paradise, and realized ordinary people lived and visited there.

This relentless wish for perfect love can go on and on, robbing us of our capacity to feel content with what's good and achievable in our lives now. This expectation must give way to friendship if we're to avoid the well-stocked wrecking yards of divorce and single parent homes. Experiencing friendship and moments of intimacy are the only goals we can ever really achieve.

If you're fortunate enough to have developed a friendship with your partner within a sexual relationship, you've achieved more than many other couples. I often visualize a couple tailgating before they

> *What is it about us that longs for a love*
> *more perfect than the one we have?*

go to a sporting event, sharing good times with each other and with their common interest. This couple becomes a unit, not just parallel partners who coexist and individually wish for something that doesn't exist.

Letting Go of the Illusion

And for Francesca, although she chose to stay in her marriage with a husband who seemed like a good man, she and Robert apparently never let go of the illusion that their love could be substantially more than the loves they'd previously experienced. The way Francesca lived her life, she felt obligation but never contentment. In her diary, she wrote how she gave her life to her husband but wanted to give eternity to Robert. For years, she secretly held on to a magical wish, spawned from infancy, that was never possible. They lived with visions of love much greater than that which exists, exiling themselves to a purgatory of hope (See Chapter 8). Both she and Robert kept it alive by not trying to live it. Yet in doing so, they denied themselves the only thing that's realistically available.

Your assignment is to *remind yourself to accept the difference between your capacity to imagine love and the reality of what you're capable of building*. There will always be a discrepancy between the two. Don't allow this discrepancy to set you on a path of longing for what no one ever achieves. There is nothing lost or worth grieving for. No one achieves ideal love. Learn how to build a friendship with your partner and practice contentment.

We will talk more about realistic expectations for love in the next chapter.

But Oh! The blessing it is to have a friend to whom one can speak fearless on any subject; with whom one's deepest as well as one's most foolish thoughts come out simply and safely. Oh, the comfort— the inexpressible comfort of feeling safe with a person—having neither to weigh thoughts nor measure words, but pouring them all right out, just as they are, chaff and grain together; certain that a faithful hand will take them and sift them, keep what is worth keeping, and then with the breath of kindness blow the rest away.

DINAH MARIA MULOCK CRAIK (1826–1887), A LIFE FOR A LIFE, 1866

14

Love is Not a Constant

Ah, the feeling of a new love—unlike any other experience. It's a feeling we secretly hope can be resurrected in its full glory throughout our lives.

Yet for many, this hope for a special love turns to feelings of despair *if* they become resigned to the reality of what they have, when they believe they'll never again love in this way.

But new love is a special, powerful form of happiness. In the beginning, it nearly consumes us and our lives seem to take a turn for the better. This pristine union effortlessly glides along; a dinner becomes exquisitely exciting, a telephone call enchanting, a walk never-ending. We're on our most exemplary behavior. We dress with purpose. Our yearning builds to a crescendo. Our feelings permeate an inordinate amount of our waking and sleeping thoughts. We make love with abandon. Hope cascades unchallenged. The focus on our partner goes uncontested and extended separations become tortuous. We're in love.

The quickness with which we fall in love when a match is found should give us pause to wonder. The feeling builds with such swiftness that even the most rational and discerning lover stands helpless in the face of these emotions. We "fall" in love and cannot help it... nor should we try to prevent it. At this time, the most we hope to achieve in rational thought is something like "...oh lord; what you do to me! This is nice but, who are you?"

Who Are You?

"Who are you?" That's the great mystery. The unanswered question. A learned professor of mine, the late James Framo, Ph.D., would say, "The real thrill in marriage is discovering just whom you married." Over time, we learn a great deal more about this person and why we were attracted to him or her. After all, the passion experience in the beginning is brief compared to the number of years in a marriage. We know so much more about our partners after five, ten, or twenty years. But initially, we need to ask, "Just what or whom were we initially in love with?" Certainly not the same partner we'd come to know after decades of companionship. If we contrast the early stages of intimacy with the less amorous reality of a lasting relationship, we gain much insight into ourselves. But more on this when we explore "Your Partner is a Reflection of Who You Are" in Chapter 15.

A Wish for Perfect Love

When we fall in love, we awaken a powerful feeling: the wish for perfect love that Francesca and countless others experience. We've had these feelings all our lives; however, only in an intimate relationship are they reawakened in their full intensity. The wish for a perfect love lies dormant in childhood until we encounter our first love relationship. In every previous relationship—with siblings, friends, classmates, and parents—the struggle involved in give and take precludes the dream long before we form our earliest intimate attachment. This struggle with "good and bad" exploded in our early childhood relationships. They frequently melted down in fights that were forgotten later that same day.

It's not until we experience our first love, however, that this wish for perfect love emerges. An unearthing of this powerful desire promises fulfillment and we ascend into epiphany. This is our first love—unlike anything we'll ever experience again—the cherished longings for a perfect union unknowingly dreamed as an infant.

This dream of perfect love— conceived but not verbalized—incubates during infancy and tenaciously holds on throughout our lives. As babies, we had dreams without words. Dreams unencumbered by reason or limits—countless unconscious dreams of perfection and blissfulness. Pure feeling.

Form Bonds with the World

These pure feelings provide the impetus to form important bonds with the outside world, initially with our mothers and fathers, affecting later development. Pure feeling to be molded by the cultural norms through childhood; pure feeling untempered by a clash with reality; a necessary time without demands for reciprocation.

This exists during infancy, which is a time when our needs become fulfilled without ever having to ask. If we wanted to be fed, for example, we became cranky and cried. We felt hunger but we didn't yet have the words to ask for food. Like magic, someone seemed in tune with our feelings of hunger and we got fed. The link between need and fulfillment was uncomplicated and magical. We needed something and couldn't ask; nevertheless it was fulfilled. We could fully immerse ourselves instantly in all our feelings: joy, frustration, con-

> *Love is not constant or unconditional.*
> *Indeed, commitment is the only*
> *constant we're capable of.*

tentment, anger. Those around us both allowed and participated in it. As adults, we miss this devotion. (See Chapter 16, "The Golden Fantasy" for more on this.)

From this time in early infancy came an expectation that can never be fulfilled—the expectation for perfect love. It is a wish to find someone who can reconnect us to that perfect love. Constantly promised in our contemporary culture's portrayal of romantic love, experiencing perfect love is desired by many. This wish stalks us in adulthood and obstructs our ability to feel contentment. It gives rise to notions that love is a constant when it's not. Love is not constant or unconditional. Indeed, commitment is the only constant we're capable of. The acceptance of this reality makes contentment possible. The perfect love of our earliest relationship with our mother was just an illusion—a necessary illusion at that time but an illusion nevertheless.

Mom Wasn't Perfect

We never saw mom moan with reluctance to get out of bed at 4:30 am, having just fallen asleep. Rarely does an infant detect mom's anger because she controls it as an act of devotion (despite continual crying). The infant isn't aware of mom's occasional feelings of ambivalence about the sacrifices she made, such as changes to her body and perhaps postponement of her career. Not conveying this to the infant denotes a significant act of love. Love that's not perfect, but surely good enough.

In psychotherapy with my clients, I can hear them tenaciously cling to their wish for perfect love. Almost every married person wonders if he or she made a mistake in selecting a life partner. The fact that they attribute this disappointment to selecting the wrong partner points to the presence of this insidious wish. This rationale preserves the wish for a perfect love that no one can achieve. A mistake can be rectified; however, the reality that no one attains perfect love can't be changed. *Acceptance* that this kind of love can't be found and is never sustained is the only hope for feeling *contentment*.

As a culture, we will continue to experience the high level of divorce and missed opportunity for contentment until we more widely accept the limits of love in marriage. It is only in the post World War II western world (when greater affluence no longer made the family structure an economic necessity) that we've had the luxury of considering all marriage possibilities. We expect fulfillment and love today. Along with this consideration of the possibilities, which are indeed considerable, must come an acceptance of the limitations.

Getting Real

So just what do we get from love in a healthy, ongoing marriage? An aging rock icon, Mick Jagger, would say, "You get what you need." It boils down to three categories of feelings, despite the prevailing culture's propensity to convince us otherwise. In a good marriage, *each day* we can expect to feel:

- *5 minutes of love*
- *15 minutes of feelings ranging from ambivalence to hate*
- *a whopping 23 hours and 40 minutes of indifference!*

Commitment is constant; love isn't. To confuse this is to adopt an expectation that love and marriage can be something they're not. So when you reflexively say "I still love him" or "I still love her," ask yourself if you're referring to the commitment you maintain or an actual feeling of love at that moment. Although feelings of love aren't constant, we certainly want to believe otherwise.

In good marriages, most people experience their five-minute daily allotment of loving feelings as a momentary appreciation for something their partner did or a quality they have. For a minute, it flows through us, infusing an essential part of our world with hope and contentment.

The 15-minute category of "ambivalence to hate" is racked up each time we swallow some contrived ideal of perfect love. This is the ambivalence. Unreasonable romantic wishes by women and excessive physical attraction to women's bodies by men are common fantasies in this category. At the other end of this continuum, but still in the same category, are the feelings of hate experienced when we become embroiled in marital spats. We're fulfilling the latter part of our vows "for better or for worse."

And for the 23 hours and 40 minutes of feelings of indifference? This is by far the largest emotional occurrence associated with marriage. How could it be any different? If we could possibly maintain feelings as intense as the relationships depicted by the movie and advertising industry, we would have neither the energy or will to accomplish anything else in our lives.

Struggle with Marriage and Intimacy

In marriage, we encounter our most deeply held wishes and unconscious dreams. It taps into a part of ourselves that we need for our individual emotional well being while providing the foundation for marriage and the family.

We are at a time in Western Civilization's development when we are struggling with our expectations for marriage and intimacy. Your assignment is to realize this struggle by fully acknowledging the depth of your longing while accepting the limits of the intimate relationship. Only then can you experience the more prevalent feelings of contentment.

It's time to "get real" and pursue what's good and achievable in marriage...contentment and friendship. Practice contentment. Build a friendship with your spouse.

Security is mostly a superstition. It does not exist in nature,
nor do the children of men as a whole experience it.
Avoiding danger is no safer in the long run than outright exposure.
Life is either a daring adventure, or nothing.

HELEN KELLER (1880–1968), THE OPEN DOOR

15

⚬⚬⚬

Your Partner is a Reflection of Who You Are

I *married the wrong person.* We tend to entertain this thought at times; that's normal. But for some people, it's a nagging source of doubt and despair. They fear they've made a lifelong mistake they must live with.

My work repeatedly reminds me how the person we marry is no accident. In relationship after relationship, I can see the continuity between each person's childhood and whom they "choose" to fall in love with.

For example, if mom and dad were not particularly close with each other, then you're less likely to pick a spouse who wants a lot of closeness. If your mom told you what to think, do, act, wear, and anticipate at every turn, you're likely to fall in love with someone willing to play this role for you. What maintains this continuity? What precludes an ability to freely choose whom we marry? It's this: *The opportunity to pick up where we leave off in critically important aspects of our relationships with our parents.*

Why do we do this? Because it's the only way we know how to receive and give love. The way we give and receive love is unique. What *isn't* unique is the powerful need to feel love. The need to feel love is a powerful and driving force that shapes goals and activities throughout our lives. The attainment of money, beauty, marriage, children, friendships, family, and power in its myriad forms is motivated by this need for love. Much effort is devoted to its pursuit.

Therefore, in finding love, we reveal (albeit unconsciously) aspects of how our emotional self has been formed. This includes *how much* love we can give and receive, and *how and when* this love is to be given and received.

Exquisitely Correct Choice

Yes, the person you fall in love with reveals how, when, and where you're comfortable becoming intimate. That person mixes in with your strengths, your uttermost fears, and your deeply held wishes. In many ways, the person you pick is an exquisitely correct choice. You may not have a viable or functional relationship, but your choice of partner isn't a mistake, despite fears of picking the wrong person. You're not deceived by the initial good impression your new lover makes. Your choice is not a product of your naiveté or tender years.

Rather, falling in love is an opportunity to realize love from the only type of person you could receive it from. Not just anyone would do. All types of love were really not within your "tastes" of possible choices. Potential mates offering a more self-disclosing love might not have felt "right." Perhaps you wouldn't find the traditional relationship in which the roles of husband and wife are closely defined acceptable.

This opportunity can only be realized if you and your spouse have the courage to undertake the journey that relationships must make. It's only possible when you *stop* trying to resurrect the early love you once had and work on becoming friends.

Similar to the discussions in "Love is not a Constant" and "Minutes of Love," Hendrix[1] lowers the expectations for feelings of love. He would say that the journey isn't about love, but about an opportunity for you and your spouse to heal the wounds and other unfinished business taken into your marriage. Central to this healing (and why your spouse is right for you) is *the potential* to empathically understand your wounds. This is what makes that person superbly correct for you. Countless times I have heard myself and my colleagues observe this premise of why a couple is together. The dysfunction that frustrates the couple—and it surely exists—is evidence of their failed journey. Failure to make progress on this journey, along with mistaken expectations about love, creates the doubt about marrying the wrong person. But the person you married was a tailored match for you; he or she represented the only place you could possibly know love. The opportunity to understand and to be understood empathetically is what creates feelings of love that you would recognize.

Michael and Janie

Because Michael struggled with his own lessons of intimacy and love, his marriage relationship had to undertake a journey that would involve a new understanding and change by Janie. His lack of progress with this journey (i.e., figuring out why he picked Janie) threatened to lead to separation and divorce. Like many, Michael was troubled by the persistent thought that Janie was not right for him. He'd already concluded they met (during their junior year in college) when they were too young to marry.

Michael was troubled with the thought that now he had made his choice and sealed it in marriage, and it was too late to rectify the mistake. This thought haunted him. Janie could feel Michael's steady emotional retreat. When he began talking about a trial separation several months after his sexual interest evaporated, Janie became frightened and called me for an appointment.

As usual at the outset of couple's therapy, Michael refused to attend the first two appointments. (Has some research psychologist quantified the percentage of wives versus husbands who initiate couples therapy? In my experience, 90 percent of the time the wife calls. It's no real surprise to acknowledge that men have trouble asking for help. Michael was no different. Left up to him, his marriage would have gone down in the burning wreckage of divorce.)

To avoid getting a one-sided picture of their marriage, I telephoned Michael and asked him to attend one session. He agreed. During our first meeting, I told him I could see why he felt his marriage was unfulfilling. I added that if it were me, I would get out of this marriage but I wouldn't have waited as long! I actually meant it, assuming that my spouse and I couldn't have improved such an unfulfilling relationship.

With those words, I could feel him relax. He knew I wouldn't pressure him to remain in a relationship that caused him to feel hopeless and empty. Michael felt supported. More importantly for him and Janie, he also felt a measure of curiosity—a feeling neither he nor Janie expected.

Understandably, Janie's anxiety rose perceptibly in this session. I knew, however, that our previous two sessions had built a bridge of trust and Janie would be OK. She felt hopeful that Michael had agreed to talk. This was positive and Janie knew it. I had to reach him before he went further with the divorce, and thus deliberately joined with him at the outset.

I've learned that a marriage is rarely over until the final papers are signed. I've learned to listen for that glimmer of hope beneath the years of anger, loneliness, frustration, and rejection; all the things this kind of pain is made of. People wait too long to ask for help. The debris of unresolved issues and frustration accumulates, finally forcing many to run for divorce. Only a few to seek help. This is unfortunate and unnecessary.

Every marital crisis is a plea screamed by couples who cannot reconcile the discrepancy between what they *now* have with what they *once* had. At times, I've been the lone supporter of a marriage that neither partner wanted in a given moment. If they have children, I think about their kids and draw strength. If they don't have children and really shouldn't be divorcing, I think about the pain they'll both endure only to arrive at a similar place years later when lessons in life go unlearned. So I manipulate and make strategic moves to get people to slow down enough to understand.

Definitely some marriages shouldn't remain intact. They won't work no matter how much therapy the couple receives. People in these relationships often tell me they knew it wasn't "right" the day they got married; one or both weren't ready.

Don't Know How to Be Married

However, the vast majority of divorces today are unnecessary. They suffer from the fact that *most people do not know how to be married* rather than the widely held fear that they married the wrong person. We get married today by the seat of our pants. Who teaches us how to select a partner and how to be married? No one. We make the most important decision in our lives on a wing and a prayer. At times I've wondered if the arranged marriages of yesteryear would fare better than how we do it today.

Unlike some of my colleagues who are loathe to influence some of their patient's decisions, I will—when the only alternative is to stand by while they self destruct. Avoiding undo influence is ethical, wise, and prudent. But when it comes to marriage or raising children, I participate in their decision-making process. Indeed, I'd be doing them a disservice by not getting them to slow down and look at a largely unconscious decision process involving some of the most powerful feelings we all harbor. The chapters "Romantic Ideals that Hurt" and "Love is Not a Constant" discuss how oblivious we can be about who we fall in love with and why. Knowing this, I do everything possible to dispel any clouded notions so that, at the very least, my clients don't repeat the same mistakes. Many times however, their marriage can be saved. In these circumstances, people in marriages delivered from the brink of dissolution face the irony that almost losing their marriage proved to be the catalyst in their building a marriage that is more satisfying.

In situations more severe than Janie and Michael's, I might be even more assertive. I might suggest that the spouse in Michael's position file for divorce. In California, it takes a minimum of six months to complete a divorce. Filing the initial paperwork sets the clock ticking. It can also take the pressure off to save the marriage because, once the clock's ticking, both partners "try on" how it feels to dissolve the marriage. It begins to take on a reality previously unseen. Raising the children, dividing finances, losing their home and friends—experiencing these things can be sobering. This doesn't happen when one spouse pursues the other to decide to stay together. All this is an attempt to provide an emotional place where they can begin to talk about *why and how* they do this thing we call marriage.

As the clock begins ticking toward dissolution in six months, I ask for a commitment from them to spend this time taking a hard look at why this marriage is dissolving. I encourage, cajole, push, and at times anger the couple into a level of honesty far exceeding anything they've previously revealed. To do otherwise would be negligent.

Our working contract spells out that at any point, if either wants out because it seems hopeless, I will help them end it. The agreed-upon minimal goal is to understand what went wrong as fully as possible so they can avoid repeating similar mistakes in future relationships. Any clinical psychologist in practice long enough could tell you about the similarities between ex-spouse and subsequent partners for those who fail to fully appreciate the dynamics underlying with whom we fall in love with. This is why who we pick is indeed a reflection of who we are.

Our Second Session

All of my suggestions didn't fall on deaf ears for Janie and Michael. Michael was curious, bright, and game. In the first session, I'd set the framework to getting out of this marriage and said I would help him and Janie when he left. That freed us to talk. Here's how our second session began.

"What did you like about Janie when you first met?" I asked Michael.

"Well, it's been so long. But I guess I was attracted to her because she was pretty, very bright, and she was sweet."

"Pretty" doesn't help me to understand that much about what was at the basis of his attraction to her. His characterization of her as "sweet" is possibly loaded with who he is. That is, the unconscious underpinning he still maintains as a prerequisite to intimacy. "Very bright" may contain his hopes and unrealized promise for this couple now in their late thirties, I quickly surmised.

"Michael, go with this for a few minutes and let's see if it has anything that might help us. Get a feeling for this question and please... just speculate. The question is, What made Janie sweet? What was it about her?"

Michael thought for a moment and replied, "Well, when we were in our third or fourth years of college, the dorm advisors called a floor meeting concerning late night noise. I forget what the incident

> *Many people feel that they married the wrong person. The problem really is that most people don't know how to be married.*

was about but a friend of Janie was getting unfairly attacked by a number of other students. They were pinning a lot more of the blame on Janie's friend than she deserved. I remember how Janie came to her rescue first by speaking up. I liked that."

"Had you begun to date yet?" I asked Michael.

"No... soon after I think."

As Janie listened quietly to this story, I wasn't sure if she had previously heard Michael's thoughts about this time years ago. She jumped in.

"You said something to me about that dorm meeting, Michael, on the way to the cafeteria. You were angry how they scapegoated her and we continued to talk in the cafeteria line and through dinner and the evening. I missed a class that afternoon because I liked you and I was interested in you."

"So Michael, what does sweet mean to you based on your warm remembrances of Janie?" I asked.

"I'm not sure what you're asking."

"Well, would you say she was kind?"

"Yes."

"Gentle?"

"Sure."

"Concerned about how other people feel?"

"O.K."

"How about assertive?"

"No. Assertive isn't what comes to mind when I think of her as sweet."

Michael broke eye contact and looked down. I sensed feelings of guilt and perhaps embarrassment as he pondered the implication.

"Do you perceive Janie as assertive today?"

"No. She needs to be more assertive," he stated with a softer voice. "She lets her employer walk on her, her family, and sometimes the kids."

Michael was becoming aware of what the selection of his partner says about him.

"Michael," I said, "it's important that you go easy on yourself right now. It's more important that we discover these hidden needs that everyone has than it is to place blame, especially on you. You're doing a good job staying open. But be easy on yourself."

"O.K."

"Well, so at this point in your marriage, do you find Janie's lack of assertion annoying or irritating?" I asked.

"Irritating," Michael again said softly while he glimpsed at Janie to assess her reaction. Michael realized that the very thing that attracted him to Janie years ago back in college was now the source of his increasing despair and growing desire to find the "right person." He married Janie because she was gentle and nurturing. This was a crucial prerequisite for him. He decided that the first time he realized his mom was not as empathic toward his dad as he wished her to be during his childhood.

In an individual session later, Michael uncovered that he felt his dad to be downtrodden and at times emotionally abandoned by his mother. Janie was nice. Janie was sweet. He wished so much for his mom to be nicer to the dad he loved. A woman like Janie was now in his cards. When Janie jumped up to protect her friend, it clicked in such a way that Michael became immediately attracted to her loyalty and kindness—very important traits to Michael. These traits had to be very strong in a woman to alleviate the fear of emotional abandonment. A woman who was stronger (what he now wanted Janie to be) would have frightened Michael during his college years. Too close to his mother's style. But now he needed Janie to be stronger. Janie needed to be stronger for herself as well.

Michael now knew what his withdrawal from Janie was about. In a subsequent session, it became necessary to mobilize Janie. To do this, Michael had to be honest with Janie, with how he felt about her

in the company of other people. Some people may have characterized this level of honesty as brutal. In my experience, nothing is
more brutal than being stuck in a divorce you didn't want. Their discussion about Michael's recent company party proved to be pivotal.

"You always leave me standing there alone at these parties while
you are off talking to everyone else," Janie complained.

"You do fine," Michael protested. "You know a lot of the people
and their wives that I work with."

"Sometimes I think you are embarrassed of me," she revealed.

"Of course not." Michael quickly responded, not wanting to hear
what she said or felt. I jumped in.

"Michael, let's go with this for a few minutes. Wanting to protect
Janie shows you're caring... however, I don't think you are really
helping Janie."

Michael drew a breath that seemed to steady him. On some level,
he knew where this was leading.

"Is there anyone at these company parties you feel wouldn't do
well with Janie? Or perhaps a person you wouldn't want Janie to
have to deal with?"

Michael thought for a moment and came up with a definitive
answer.

"Margo can be a bit much. She's an unbelievable producer who
takes delight from beating her male counterparts. She repeatedly
makes a point of showing disdain for women that she calls 'dizzy.'"

"Dizzy?"

"Yeah, more traditional. Clothes, kids, movies. Her attitude is 'get
a life,'" Michael said.

"OK, I understand. But, do you admire or like anything about
Margo?"

"Well... like I said, she's a top producer."

Janie correctly sensed some withholding and jumped in. *"She's
also pretty, Michael,"* she stated emphatically. Michael could only

sigh. This was courageous. Most men would have thrown up a blizzard of obfuscation to prevent the emergence of the frightening reality that was at hand.

"You're embarrassed of me, Michael," Janie said with tears whose reality burned a newly found consciousness into her cheeks.

"No, I am not," Michael said out of a combination of empathy and self-preservation. I couldn't let this stop here.

"So how would you feel about an encounter between Janie and Margo?" I asked Michael.

Michael's response couldn't change the perception that Janie held. After all, she was right. Michael was embarrassed of Janie meeting certain people and Margo was one of them. Janie now knew the truth about herself and her dissolving marriage with Michael.

Michael now realized the very thing that attracted him to Janie years ago, was now feeding his increasing despair and desire to find the right person. If he tried to go out and find the *right person* today, he would still be attracted to a soft, non-assertive woman. Just not Janie. The vicarious participation in Janie's softness and sweetness wasn't going to do any longer. Michael was on the verge of realizing that he wanted to be cared for by a woman who had strength but who wouldn't use this strength to slay his heart. This was a woman he could again believe in. This was a woman strong enough for Michael to reach and reveal feelings of vulnerability and need he never allowed to be soothed or fulfilled. If it was going to be Janie, then she needed to develop her strength. This meant her being able to have direction in life and a stronger sense of herself.

A Lesson in Marriage

Your assignment, derived from Janie and Michael's struggle, is to move the question beyond "Did you marry the wrong person?" to the question "Where does our marriage need to go?" Michael needed to take the risks that go with vulnerability. He had to find out if the woman he trusted slayed his heart like his mom did to his dad, or whether she responded with care and love. Janie's growth was detailed above. Whether they stayed married or divorced, their individual growth paths remained the same. They stayed married.

Michael and Janie discontinued their therapy a few months later. More than five years passed before I'd see Janie and Michael again. Janie was working full-time as a senior administrator in a medium-sized tech company. She developed a reputation for being tough but fair! People loved to work for her.

Janie not only forgave Michael for his brutal honesty but thanked him for how pivotal it had become in her life. And how Michael loved Janie. Anyone could see the admiration in his gaze for who she was and who she'd become. I was proud of this couple's courage to move together down the road their relationship had to travel.

Michael and Janie taught us something about change and being married. Farewell Michael and Janie.

---

[1] Hendrix, Harville, *Getting the Love You Want*, 1988.

Three things are necessary for salvation of man:
to know what he ought to believe;
to know what he ought to desire;
and to know what he ought to do.

ST. THOMAS AQUINAS (1225–1274), TWO PRECEPTS OF CHARITY

16

The Golden Fantasy

ebecca was a 29-year-old, married, bright, second-year law student who telephoned to arrange couples counseling. I returned her telephone call later and found her at home, studying for an exam.

"Hello."

"Hello... is Rebecca available please."

"This is Rebecca."

"Rebecca, I am Dr. Habib; did I catch you at a good time? Can you talk?"

"Yes... Yes... Thank you for calling. Let me shut the door."

"How can I help you?"

"Well, I don't know if you can. But, it has to do with communication between my husband and me. We've been married five years, and Joel and I can't always communicate."

"Hmm. OK. What happens?"

"I am trying to talk with him about something, and I know he hates it when I get serious. It pains him to listen to me. Then I get mad at him and start yelling. This causes him to check out, you know, emotionally. Which just makes me angrier. Then I am mad for a while because he doesn't seem to get it."

"Get what, Rebecca?"

"What I want. He seems to understand. But when it comes down to whether or not he'll be there... many times he's not and I end up angry again."

Rebecca and Joel

Rebecca and Joel were scheduled for an initial session early the following week. Joel was a 32-year-old, good-looking engineer who was less verbal and emotionally expressive than Rebecca. I could sense his reluctance to attend couples counseling, which is typical for the majority of men. As soon as the conversation centered on their relationship, I could feel a subtle shift in Joel's demeanor that seemed to turn inward. He became even less emotionally available than in the moments before. The question was why?

I considered the options while struggling to stay open to the unexpected. Was Joel exhibiting battle fatigue from unproductive attempts to communicate that frequently ended in criticism? Or was this a passive aggressive maneuver to gain power by thwarting her overt attempts to communicate? Perhaps he didn't know what he felt and scurried for cover when the communication threatened to expose issues he wasn't ready to acknowledge. When not seated in my office, Rebecca and Joel were only moments away from the conflict that brought them in and always left them feeling how fruitless their problem solving had become. That's how many couples unintentionally construct the walls that take their toll on the warmth and love they might otherwise share.

Initial Session

An initial therapy session for couples involves gaining understanding of their strengths and weaknesses. I frequently choose to temporarily put off their most pressing issues to stabilize their relationship and get further down the road with their therapy. We looked at how they solved problems together, at their ability to nurture each other, achieve conflict resolution, identify their own needs and feelings, and take ownership. We touch on the subject of sexual compatibility including the frequency of sexual desire, the degree of consensus in life goals, the relationships with extended families, and their respective ability to be their own person. All totaled, Rebecca and Joel had many strengths between them.

However, a recurring theme continued to emerge. It frequently culminated in a fight neither of them wanted. I could hear the underlying premise of this theme whenever they talked about something concerning the give and take necessary between two people in an intimate relationship.

The Golden Fantasy

This reoccurring theme suggested an underlying premise called the Golden Fantasy, which set them up for failure because of the inherently unrealistic expectation it contained. It functioned as a litmus test for Rebecca of Joel's love for her. See if you can hear this Golden Fantasy in the following conversation.

"Can you give me an example of when he's not there for you, Rebecca?" I asked.

"Oh, that's easy. Last week, Joel was going to the supermarket to buy this toothpaste he likes. He heard me say a few hours earlier that we were out of coffee creamer, which I'd need in the morning. Do you think he thought of that when he was at the store? No. He gets his toothpaste but I am drinking black coffee Sunday morning. This is just an example of how inconsiderate Joel can be."

"You really hate black coffee," I said to lighten the moment and keep Joel emotionally present.

"But that's not the point," she interjected.

"I know, but would he have purchased the coffee creamer if you'd asked, say, just before he left or if you'd given him a list of what you wanted?

"Yes—but do I have to ask for everything? Isn't anything common sense? I did previously mention we were out of creamer. Why isn't that enough? It makes me feel like I can't depend on him," Rebecca concluded with resignation and heartfelt disappointment.

"I understand, Rebecca. It hurts to feel like he's not there for you and to wonder if he has a fatal flaw of self absorption that'll never allow him to get outside of himself and be responsive to the modest things that you need."

"You got it," Rebecca stated.

She began to cry and Joel again looked like he was a schoolboy in trouble outside the principal's office. "If he loved me, he would know what I need " Rebecca uttered through a torrent of tears that burned in frustration and defeat. Rebecca had clearly stated the Golden Fantasy. *If he loved me he (she) would know what I need.* A fantasy that almost everyone uses as a test of their partner's love and commitment.

Needs Filled Without Asking

The truth is that no one knows what you need. The Golden Fantasy is an infant's impression of how give and take works. Consider the following description of where the fantasy begins.

When you were hungry as an infant, you didn't think, *Boy a warm one would taste good right now.* Since you hadn't acquired language, you just fussed or screamed until you were fed, held, or cared for.

> *"If he loved me, he would know what I need," Rebecca uttered through a torrent of tears that burned in frustration and defeat.*

From your perspective, it was like magic. A *warm one* indeed came along, or perhaps a hug, attention, loving, or a change of clothes if you needed it. You didn't have to ask for it. You didn't have to consciously recognize the need. You just felt a need and it was frequently met—all without you having to ask for it. Thus the Golden Fantasy: If you loved me, you would know what I need.

The other reality of that infant bliss, specifically your mother's, might have gone something like this. You screamed because you were hungry at 3:30 a.m. And, by the way, it was your third awakening that night. Mom muttered something less than loving as she unsuccessfully tried to get Dad to do this feeding. She dragged herself out of bed and said sarcastically to herself, "And he wanted a big family." But by the time she got to your room, she pulled it together and lovingly fed you after determining if you were wet. Hardly the idyllic love that is magical, but it's good enough—and all there is in the world of reality.

As an infant, you weren't aware of the normal mix of positive and negative feelings that comes with any relationship. Thankfully, the majority of moms don't take their momentary irritation out upon their children; they pull it together.

We have been indulged in years of love and tolerance necessary to raise a healthy and well-adjusted child. Yet even though we grow older and mature in many important ways, we leave our childhood with this fantasy largely intact. It's destined to emerge with its unrealistic expectations when we fall in love. In time, it collides with a different reality than what we perceived as a child. Even though it was never real with mom, we persist in hoping that it's real somewhere and with someone and can form the basis of the love we want.

Just because your spouse doesn't live up to this ideal is not proof of a fatally flawed relationship. There's no truth to the widely held fear that everyone else has a much more responsive relationship. If it wasn't for an initial mistake in partner selection, you too could drown in this sea of love. Although partners may indeed share the Golden Fantasy and use it as a yardstick to measure their relationship, it doesn't exist in reality. No one knows what you need and it's never fair to expect your partner to anticipate your needs.

Reigning in the Golden Fantasy

Your ability to accept the reality of marriage has much to do with feelings of contentment as well as the stability of the marriage over time. The following three points will remind you what is realistic in love and marriage. Your assignment is to build these suggestions into your relationship.

1. You are responsible for what you want. If you didn't ask for it, then it's no one's fault but your own.
2. Be careful of allowing expectations like the Golden Fantasy to creep into your relationship with your spouse. However, this doesn't mean you shouldn't expect to build reasonable levels of sensitivity and responsiveness with your partner.
3. As with any ideal, watch out for how you relate to it. At its best, it should provide a beacon toward which you navigate your relationship—all the while accepting and knowing that you'll never arrive at this ideal.

By definition, an ideal is a destination that entails a journey without end. At its worst, an ideal contaminates our ability to feel contentment. The Golden Fantasy is an ideal specific to those who are (or have been) in love. Don't allow it to set up expectations that are predestined for disappointment. Watch out for the subtle ways it can creep into your marriage. And don't underestimate how much progress our culture has yet to make with this unconscious wish for the Golden Fantasy.

Resolution for Joel and Rebecca

Rebecca went through a short period when she was angry at Joel for not meeting this need and at me for destroying this expectation. I understood her reaction as an abbreviated grief reaction, similar to the grief of losing a loved one. Rebecca quickly accepted this new reality and became much clearer in expressing what she wanted or what was important to her. I felt that Rebecca, like many of us, would neither become cynical or angry about love. I particularly admired her willingness to negotiate and, at times, barter for the give and take necessary in any marriage. All of this made it much more predictable and concrete for Joel. Consequently, he was able to stop the automatic retreat from serious conversation that Rebecca hated. In fact, one of the final conversations I heard between Rebecca and Joel was about when to begin their family. Be well, Rebecca and Joel.

Emancipation from error is the condition of real knowledge.

HENRI FREDERIC AMIEL (1821–1881)

17

⚫⚫

Affairs and Pretty Women

D ave was flooded with guilt. His body pulsated with the turmoil that churned inside. He'd fallen in love with a female colleague at work. But Dave was married and had two children he loved. It wasn't that he grew to dislike his wife of ten years. A woman now in her late thirties, she was showing the markings of motherhood and age. Life was comfortable and whole with Joyce and they navigated life's challenges with above average success and skill.

Rachel, in her late twenties, turned heads wherever she walked. Her auburn hair pulled into a tight bun crowning her head revealed facial features that were enchanting from any angle of view. The natural beauty of her almond-shaped eyes, with only a delicate amount of makeup, could distract the most focused man at an initial encounter. Her business attire, appropriate and understated, couldn't conceal her ample breasts, slender legs, and curving silhouette that persisted in most men's thoughts long after she walked away. When she showed interest in Dave that was casual and playful at first, he hadn't given a thought to the vulnerability he was bringing forth, yet its effect now wracked his body. An after-work drink flowed into a sexual encounter and the ecstasy he felt during these interludes overshadowed the approaching conflict. Neither of them faced the impending distress until two weeks of liaisons ignited the compelling feelings of early love.

Dave knew he had a problem. What he felt with Rachel was intense and powerful. The thought of letting her go seemed impossible. On the other hand, his relationship with Joyce was comfortable and fidelity was necessary to continue being part of the daily lives of his children he deeply cared for. Dave wanted Rachel, but he cared for his wife and family. He couldn't fathom any loss of time away from his children. Sharing early mornings in Mom and Dad's bed, the excitement of their accomplishments and concern over their struggles unfolded into a daily rhythm he enjoyed. Any decision to leave meant colossal loss and the thought of telling them he was departing became unthinkable. This dilemma wasn't worth the pain he was enduring. Joyce had yet to learn of this affair although she sensed something was wrong and noticed his distraction and distance. Dave had to shoulder the tribulation alone.

Men are Vulnerable

Dave fell into this relationship with Rachel because he retained his magical view of physical beauty. Men unceasingly play these fantasies in their thoughts—thoughts that define the image of the modern-day but mythical female goddess defined by large breasts and a slender body.

Today, a man's relationship to women's breasts constitutes a culturally reinforced fetish. They became a facet of love that goes beyond any reality of what having access to them would mean. After all, they're just breasts on a person. But a man's reaction is one of awe and veneration that can be universally heard in any male group absent the modulating effect of a women's presence.

When Irving "Magic" Johnson, the Los Angeles Lakers' basketball player, was diagnosed with AIDS, he revealed similar choices men encounter in the high visibility world of most celebrities. In an honest and poignant admission, he described the daily mix of private hotel rooms, distant cities, and women "groupies" assertively pursuing these young men wherever they traveled. These men's experiences raise an interesting question. That is, given a similar opportunity, what percentage of men would decline a clandestine affair with a physically beautiful woman who came on strong? I suspect the vast majority of men would fail this test and find this offer irresistible. Possibly the lack of opportunity protects the majority of men today who would fare no better than Magic Johnson or my writhing patient Dave.

Great Dilemma for Men

The lure of the physically gifted woman presents perhaps the single greatest challenge or dilemma for men; it is especially true in partner selection. It lies in one's ability to avoid being blinded by this single positive trait at the exclusion of a host of other issues. These issues will certainly prove more important as time uncovers the person cloaked in the pretty face. The fact that men project so many positive feelings on a woman's physical beauty reveals deeply held and heartfelt wishes for perfect love mentioned in other chapters. Women engage in the same process of projection, but the wish is for unrealistic levels of romantic love discussed in the chapters "Romantic Ideals that Hurt" and "Love is not a Constant." What we have in reality, however, even in the best of relationships, will never be equal to what

> *The lure of the physically gifted woman presents perhaps the single greatest challenge or dilemma for men.*

we're capable of imagining. The male version of this wish can be seen in our infatuation with physically beautiful woman.

Women play a role in this process, although their ability to focus on more realistic relational dynamics appears to be stronger. To some degree, women rely on their physical attributes for influence and control. Those who are especially attractive and unwilling to relinquish being the object of this adulation are prone to eating disorders, excessive exercise, and multiple cosmetic surgeries as discussed in "Getting Older." To the extent a woman relies on her physical beauty, she is stunting the possibilities for being independent and fully realized while setting up an inevitable conflict with her aging self.

Find Out Who They Are

For men, your assignment is to approach a woman you find physically attractive while deliberately saying to yourself, "OK, this is nice, but who are you?"

In doing so, you have a chance to realistically evaluate what you are becoming involved in and acquire a sense of what being in a relationship with this woman will feel like five, ten, and fifteen years from now. Furthermore, women prefer to be appreciated for their personhood rather than their bodies.

For the married man, it's foolish to disrupt your family life for the younger woman in a desperate attempt to reacquire what you mistakenly assume you cannot live without. Beautiful women are only people—people with personalities that may be easy or extremely difficult to undertake life's passages with. If you haven't dated long enough to know that initial attractions dissolve into coping with that person's whole being, then you're not ready for marriage. If you married young before experience could temper the lure of physical attraction and you harbor silent disappointment, get over it. You're not missing anything you don't already have and your disappointment is interfering with your ability to feel contentment today.

Dave's Story

Dave never left his wife. Rachel walked away and mercifully put an end to the relationship when it became apparent he was too conflicted to leave his wife in the near future. I suspect she also learned a costly, painful lesson about getting involved with married men. Dave remained in therapy for an additional six months and we talked about life's limitations and simple pleasures. As I advised, he never told his wife about his unfaithfulness. I rarely see value in coming clean on these issues knowing how painful it would be for Joyce. I opted to push Dave into learning how to protect himself from careless choices like these and to more fully appreciate Joyce, his children, and the life they built. The last few times I saw Dave, he was much more cautious with his flirting and seemed content to admire beauty from a safer distance.

Pythagoras was misunderstood, and Socrates, and Jesus, and Luther, and Copernicus, and Galileo, and Newton, and every pure and wise spirit that ever took flesh. To be great is to be misunderstood.

RALPH WALDO EMERSON (1803–1882), SELF RELIANCE

18

⤳⤳

He Wants Sex and
She Wants to be Hugged

D rew immediately got up from the dining room table when he saw the plastic soda bottle run dry on his wife Diane. He came back with a full bottle that hissed when he twisted its cap, filled a glass with ice, and then lightly ran his fingers through her hair before returning to his dinner. Diane could feel her initial appreciation fade into feelings of duty and pressure to have sex later that evening. After fourteen years of marriage, this meant Drew wanted to make love tonight. She knew this wasn't fair but she'd already decided she didn't want to have intercourse... and he hadn't even asked yet.

This scenario occurred more and more frequently in the past seven or so years. Drew didn't know just how much conflict Diane was feeling about their sexual relationship. He just assumed she was tired. Buried beneath this all-too-easy explanation were his growing feelings of rejection and loneliness.

The pressure to have sex rendered it as an act of duty for Diane. This destined almost every sexual encounter as unsatisfactory for her and strictly a physical release for him. It didn't bring them closer.

In fact, Drew felt subtly rejected. He was incapable of putting into words the abandonment and feelings of inadequacy he felt. He began to dislike his greater need for sex. If the truth be told, this impasse posed the greatest flaw in a relationship that otherwise worked well.

Diane couldn't understand why Drew wanted to have so much sex. She sensed that he'd want it twice or three times a week if she had a matching desire or promoted these encounters. To head off the tension that would arise from him wanting more sex, Diane began to behave less sexually to stem any misinterpretation and pressure she felt. The changes were subtle, but her attire became more conservative and she undressed and dressed in private. She refrained from any erotic conversations and unconsciously drifted into gaining a few pounds.

Diane drew comfort from many of her married girlfriends who said, in one way or the other, that they could do with a lot less sex. At various times, she's heard about faked orgasm, disingenuous sounds of pleasure, the ever-present pressure to "do it." One confidante overtly wished her husband had a mistress. Other than the last woman, many of these marriages were relatively successful. Although Diane had never resorted to faking an orgasm, she learned that the practice was much more widespread than most men suspected.

That night, Drew asked to make love as Diane had suspected. She was able to respond, albeit reluctantly. When Drew attempted to manually bring her to an orgasm, she said "no" and told him it was OK for him to finish. This told Drew she wasn't really into it and again raised feelings of rejection and subtle feelings of abandonment he couldn't identify. The whole experience was over in ten minutes and Diane felt relieved she now had a one-week reprieve until the next encounter. Diane felt badly about this, but didn't know how to change it. Drew was a generous partner who cared about his wife and their sexual relationship. He attempted to talk about this aspect of their intimacy but managed to only make mildly disparaging remarks and one-liners. Diane didn't know just how much Drew supplemented intercourse with self-stimulation. He suspected that she didn't know or care. And she never objected to the occasional erotic magazine he purchased that he stashed in the back of his nightstand drawer.

Diane's self-simulation tailed off almost completely since her early thirties. She didn't self-stimulate to orgasm in Drew's presence—never a necessity since he was more than willing to accommodate her need. It seemed there was no way for Drew and Diane to reconcile their differences in desire for sexual intercourse. What used to create closeness and intimacy now precipitated tension and feelings of rejection. Otherwise, their marriage worked reasonably well.

Drew and Diane are not alone in this incompatibility in need for sexual contact. Likewise, they are equally lost about what to do about it.

The Professional Community

Most clinicians avoid the issue of sexual compatibility for both good and bad reasons. Good reasons to avoid it have to do with a prudent decision not to raise an issue that many conflicted couples can't successfully discuss. A couple who doesn't have adequate communication skills to navigate issues such as money, child rearing, family issues, work, or socializing can rarely discuss an issue as volatile as sex and expect that something constructive will come out of it. The wise psychologist delays this discussion until the immediate crisis is resolved and communication skills strengthened. It's fairly easy to do harm in couples therapy by bringing up the subject too soon—a good reason to avoid discussing differences in a couple's sexual relationship.

Bad reasons for a clinician to avoid helping a couple work on this issue include not knowing what to do. Most therapists accept as fact the underlying assumption that a woman's desire for sex will increase as sensitivity and communication improves. This is true to some extent. But the underlying assumption is that there's no difference in sexual desire between men and women. Yet there *is* a difference between most men and women—a difference that is likely to persist beyond the resolution of other issues. No doubt, there is some mileage to be gained in strengthening communication and many other issues; however, I contend this will only take a couple so far.

Women Partnering on Many Levels

Until the last few decades, the impregnable male motif was the silent, quiet image. Along with this came less flattering attributes such as controlling and repressive behaviors that have dominated most of male/female interactions for countless millenniums. The "good old days" stoked a quiet resentment and a repression of a woman's potential that did not foster partners who could develop a sexual identity. Too often, women were treated like servants rather than full participants with individual interests.

In many western cultures today, a growing plurality of men are no longer threatened by a woman capable of partnering across many levels. These men are coming to realize the win-win benefits of partnership-based relationships. I have worked with articulate and emotionally available men in relationships with women who have a lower desire for sex than they do. This challenges the underlying assumption held by most in the therapeutic community; that is, work on the communication and sensitivity issues and the frequency of desire will equalize. In fact, many couples go through couples therapy without the issue of sex ever being discussed. They often complete their couples therapy leaving this issue unaddressed

Most therapists accept as fact the underlying assumption that a woman's desire for sex will increase as sensitivity and communication improves.

and unresolved. At the core of this glaring omission is the fact that many therapists don't know what to do.

The professional community is not really talking about the incompatibility in sexual desire between men and women. We are still in an era when the whole issue of what it means to be a woman is our predominant focus. On the whole, I believe this time has been well spent and has resulted in a monumental shift from role assignment that has benefited both men and women. The time still may not be right, however, to think about how to deal with the basic incompatibility of sexual desire between men and women. I too feel some risk and thus reluctance to raise this issue, fearing unflattering judgment from my colleagues.

It's not too surprising the therapeutic community doesn't know how to deal with this issue or is even conscious of what the issue is. Many psychologists are trained in Masters and Johnson's and Kaplan's work (see Resources), all of which is quite dated. Of course, their work was groundbreaking and valuable in an era when masturbation or orgasm was never mentioned. Recently, David M. Schnarch (see Resources) has added valuable insights in critiquing this area and adding contextually informed concepts such as the "couple crucible."

However, by far the most attuned writer I have come across is Dr. Warren Farrell (see Resources) who has been ignored and at times shunned by the professional community. The therapeutic community is either largely ignorant of these issues or in collective denial of the admittedly disturbing issues raised by Dr. Farrell. Among the disturbing issues he raises is this discrepancy in sexual desire and the differences between men and women in what he calls their "primary fantasies."

According to Dr. Farrell, a woman's primary fantasy entails a desire to build home and hearth while a man's primary fantasy is to have sex with as many women as possible. These are conflicting fantasies. And, according to Farrell, a woman's fantasy is what couples adopt throughout most western cultures. It's reasonable to conclude that this strongly correlates with the discrepancy in sexual desire between men and women. However, Dr. Farrell doesn't offer an adequate solution. Although I will try, I will likely fail at providing a full and comprehensive solution to this issue. Nevertheless, I will put forth what I want to achieve in therapy with reasonably healthy couples, as I did with Drew and Diane.

Diane and Drew

Diane began individual therapy shortly after her mother died. Some understandable depression and the inevitable unresolved issues tend to surface at these times. During our early discussions, the topic of her marriage came up. She had commented how supportive Drew had been during her time of loss. However, within this context of appreciation, the difficulty with their incompatibility in frequency of sexual desire came up as an off-handed remark. (Clients in therapy often drift into areas of needed growth when they feel safe and supported, as she did here.) When Diane began to talk, she revealed the extent of pressure and resentment she felt toward Drew around this issue.

After determining that Diane wasn't overtly defensive, I asked her whether she thought Drew self-stimulated. She said she really hadn't thought about it, but that she supposed he did. She quipped that he probably didn't purchase the erotic magazines for their literary content. I noted that Diane had an easy-going but realistic view of the world that bode well for what I was going to suggest.

I asked Diane whether Drew had ever self-stimulated in her presence? When she said no, I observed an uncomfortable shift in her posture. I went on and asked, "Well, I was wondering if this might be a possible alternative to actual sexual intercourse when you know you're not interested in doing it?"

"Umm, I don't know," she began hesitantly. "I wonder if Drew would be happy with this or is he just going to want sex or get angry about this idea?"

"Well, he might find it erotic," I added, "and it might just solve the problem of him going to bed frustrated or feeling abandoned."

Diane needed time to think about this so I helped the conversation drift to another topic. At our next session, I raised the issue again. Diane had been thinking about it. She quickly asked how she should approach Drew with this suggestion. We discussed the considerable sensitivity involved in doing this and devised a casual approach with Drew that went something like this.

"Drew, I read that men never totally give up self-stimulation whether they're married or not," she stated.

Drew was immediately curious but a little defensive, not sure where this conversation was leading. "Yeah... so."

"Well, I was thinking. Would you ever do it while I was there?"

"No, why would I do that when you're there. I'd rather have sex."

"Come on Drew. I want you to do it with me."

Drew needed to be asked more than once... it felt reassuring and he understandably needed this level of support. But Drew was really intrigued with the idea, also. He asked why. Diane limited her explanation as only a sexual curiosity. More importantly, she got him to agree to try it.

The night arrived when he wanted sex and Diane reminded him about his promise. She held him as he self-stimulated while offering words of support and encouragement.

As time went on, this alternative became easier for Diane and Drew to use. Although Drew obviously preferred sexual intercourse, the option of self-stimulation decreased his frustration and the smoldering marital tension it had created. Diane also began to report feeling significantly less pressure to engage in what felt like "duty sex."

With less pressure to perform, the knee-jerk reaction she had developed toward anything sexual subsided over the course of three months. By the time we ended couples therapy, she reported a few times actually desiring the closeness offered by sexual intimacy. Diane and Drew had the courage to accept and confront their differences that many couples leave open to fester.

Getting Real about Sex and Marriage

Here are three assignments for both men and women.

For Men:

1. Let your woman into knowing what it's like to be a man. A study shows that men think about sex every three to fifteen minutes, where frequency modestly diminishes with age (Shanor, 1978)[1]. This is quite a burden and it potentially blinds us to many other areas of consideration. It's only the combination of pragmatic insight and a healthy dose of values that allow us to cope with this masculine reality. Otherwise, all men would attempt to have sex with as many women as possible. We don't need to be ashamed of this strong desire, but we do need to be conscious of how powerful a factor it can be in our lives.

2. For the most part, women will never be the sexually willing partners men fantasize about. These women do not exist. Despite how they may occasionally dress, what is watched in movies, listened to in music, seen on commercials or advertisement, or read in erotic magazines, women are not looking for sex as a pure experience. Women want to feel the contentment that a long-term relationship offers and, on the whole, don't feel sexual urges as frequently as men do.

3. Men need to expect that women will have a slow sexual warm up and frequently consent out of caring obligation or a recognition that once it gets started they'll enjoy it. Although this

isn't the sexual encounter envisioned in a man's fantasy, rest assured that you often don't fulfill her fantasies either. Deal with it and stay open to the closeness that usually unfolds. Feel the contentment that a long-term relationship offers.

For Women:

1. Note the slow sexual warm-up that later burns as genuine erotic feelings and desire. Ask for whatever you need to help this process, including foreplay or warm interactions leading up to sexual intercourse, but be open to your mate's efforts to getting it started. The woman who doesn't attempt to accommodate a man's greater need for sex has a marriage and a man that is vulnerable.

2. Try to incubate romantic and sexual thoughts throughout the day. Notice what attracts you visually or within your thoughts and fantasize. Attend to small experiences and find ways to recognize and cultivate your own sexuality.

3. It's important that you *choose* to become sexually responsive and keep this part of your relationship alive to avoid developing resentment and withdrawing. Remember that relationships entail "give and take." An active sexual relationship can help renew closeness and commitment even when communication fails or marital conflict runs high.

---

[1] Shanor, Karen. *The Shanor Study: The Sexual Sensitivity of the American Male.* New York, Dial Press. 1978. p. 103

The language of truth unadorned and always simple.

MARCELLINUS AMMIANUS, ROMAN HISTORIAN

19

Controlling Powerful Feelings:
Relationships That Work

Alicia asked Ian how he felt about the coming visit of her friend. Ian's exhale inflated his cheeks, his hand smoothed his hair and came to rest on the back of his neck. He met Alicia's patient gaze with a tint of trepidation. She remained quiet as Ian sat up straight and raised his shoulders by pushing both hands into his thighs. In a moment, his breathing became more rhythmic. He relaxed his torso and responded, "I guess I am not looking forward to it. But that's probably no big surprise to you, is it?"

"No, Ian. Every time I mention it, you seem like you are in excruciating pain."

"I am sorry, Alicia. I know this visit is very important for you."

"What's the problem, Ian?"

This relationship was a pleasure to watch. This early forties couple have been married for fourteen years and their relationship was working very well. They requested couples counseling for growth and enhancement rather than a crisis that precipitates most therapy.

"I don't like being around your friend. She's always so proper and appropriate, I feel like I can't relax. It's a major risk to be spontaneous and how she sets a tone where everyone, including you, begin doing the same thing. It makes me feel uptight," Ian moaned.

"What can I do, Ian? I'm looking forward to the chance to spend time with her and share our home. But I'd like to help you so that I don't see you hating every moment of her visit."

Earned High Marks

This couple already has earned high marks for several things. In many relationships, Ian might not have even begun to speak before Alicia would have reacted with hurt for Ian not caring about her needs or what was important to her. Of course, what she wants is reasonable and appropriate. During this brief but potentially explosive interaction, Alicia kept her feelings under control by focusing on Ian. Her emotions didn't come crashing in as Ian attempted to put words to his feelings of reluctance. When they do come crashing in (which is the case with too many couples), it's called "chaotic regression."

Controlling powerful feelings is the hallmark of successful interaction. It is something most of us routinely provide for inconsiderate coworkers, insensitive supervisors, and remiss friends. We allow them latitude for mistakes and anger.

In most intimate couples' relationships, this margin of tolerance can be anywhere from nonexistent to too narrow. By nonexistent, I mean that the smaller percentage of married people tolerate too much and are frequently abused or taken advantage of. When their tolerance is too narrow, they expect their spouses to be perfectly responsive to their feelings. This is far more prevalent, and unlike Ian and Alicia. Chaotic regression isn't the norm for Ian and Alicia. If it was, they would have gotten nowhere and Ian would have been a reluctant participant for countless holidays and future gatherings.

They would have never learned what made it so uncomfortable for Ian to be around her friend. If uncontrolled regression was their pattern, the conversation would have perhaps drowned in Alicia's tearful need for reassurance that her desires were indeed important to Ian. He might have reassured her of it while prematurely promising to have a better attitude about the visit. His promise would have been motivated to avoid further conflict. Or it could have stemmed from feelings of guilt rather than from true resolution of his discomfort with her friend. On some level, Alicia would have felt the insincerity of it and the conversation would have ended with her not quite feeling satisfied with what she received. But their relationship is able to handle the regression much better than that.

Being There for Each Other

In the two minutes it took for this conversation to unfold, Alicia was able to push her legitimate needs aside so that this relationship could problem-solve. Two minutes. Time that we often give to irate customers or repeatedly abusive family members who certainly deserve less of our patience than does our most significant other. Both Ian and Alicia prove that they can handle the emotional regression that characterizes the intimate relationship by pushing their immediate feelings aside to be emotionally receptive to the other. This is what it means to be there for each other.

The dialogue continued. "Why does she have to set the tone in our home? I'll be damned if I allow her to do it on our turf," Ian stated.

Seeing an opportunity to reestablish the primacy of this relationship and address how emotionally abandoned Ian feels in her friend's presence, I interjected, "She doesn't, Ian. What if Alicia helped you talk to each other and your guest like you always do. You know, if you were to say something more self-disclosing or even controversial and Alicia made sure it didn't go down in a ball of flames."

"Yeah, that would be great," Ian stated.

"But would you want to do that, Alicia?" Ian asked. "Do you think you would recognize it when you're getting pulled into her uptight tone?"

"I'll probably need help staying aware when I drift into her 'being appropriate' game. I don't know why I get sucked into that," she said.

Because Alicia was able to control her own regression, we learn that Ian feels emotionally alone in the presence of her friend. In essence, he loses the wife he has come to know when her friend visits. No one ever intended to exclude him, of course, but a dynamic laid down years ago continues to operate today. In this instance, it is a process where being appropriate somehow became more valued than authenticity and spontaneity. Alicia later recognized that this process came from her family history.

Now, Ian is more invested in the visit because he's intrigued at the prospect of them being presented as a united couple. Alicia and Ian might discuss issues that draw some discomfort. Occasionally, they'll remain united as a couple and venture into territory that might widen the terrain available for sharing when they are with her friend or family.

We also noted how Ian was able to make an observation about Alicia's behavior when he asked, "*Could you even recognize when you're getting pulled into that uptight game?*" Alicia didn't react defensively by immediately feeling criticized. Her defensive response could have been, "Yes, I think I can Ian (indignantly)" or she could have immediately reacted by denying the pattern and saying, "I don't do that." Instead, she uses an outside observation to spur insights into herself by asking, "I don't know why I do that?"

With that statement, Alicia owns that habit rather than becoming defensive about it. If she was unsure whether Ian's observations were correct, she might just as well have asked, "You know, I don't see it that way. What do you think you're seeing?"

Being Transparent With Each Other

This too would have been a good question to ask. Other people can always see our process better than we can because of their objectivity. Allowing this to happen is what it means to become transparent with each other.

Few couples avail themselves of this capacity to become transparent with each other because they're feeling attacked. It's as if they do not trust each other, at some basic level, to permit each other to be their external observer. Valuable insights are rejected and, when offered, only serve to elicit emotional conflict and distance. Much is either left unsaid, unheard, or both. In time, the couple struggles with emotions of emptiness as they feel the need for more intimacy and fulfillment in their relationship. They never realize how they have systematically erected the distance they now endure.

The Friend's Visit

The visit went well and Ian remarked that he'd be willing to reciprocate by visiting her home. At times throughout her friend's stay, Alicia gave Ian opportunities to raise topics and engage in exchanges that would have never unfolded in other visits. This helped her friend relax and open up. They discussed with curiosity if they could maintain this less rigid pattern when at her large family gatherings.

Resolution of this couple dynamic would have never been possible without Alicia's effort to control her regression. Keep up the good work, Alicia and Ian. I often think of the example you set for many other couples I have worked with.

Controlling powerful feelings is the hallmark of successful interaction.

We're still lost but making time.

YOGI BERA (1925–   )

20

Twelve Things Women Should Avoid in Men

When Ryan began therapy, she was 28 years old. She had been married at 21 for a brief two years when her husband declared that they married too young. Ryan felt enormous pain and embarrassment when he ended their marriage—one that barely got started. She used to trust her feelings and judgment but with this breakup, she began questioning everything about herself and her marriage.

After the breakup, Ryan noticed what had become a familiar pattern in her relationships with men including her ex-husband. This is what she wanted to work on in therapy. She was attracted to men who were sensitive, easygoing, warm, and cooperative. So far, this sounds good. However, the common pattern was this: Their lives would be going nowhere. These men were chronic underachievers who rarely took a stand on anything, whether it was a statement about themselves or a determination to go after a career or a passionate interest in life. Although these men were non-confrontational and relatively easy to live with, Ryan always felt she carried a greater part of the load than they did, both emotionally and financially. She felt like she was a magnet for "little boys" who wanted to be mothered.

We began to explore how she felt about more traditional men who were assertive, powerful, and confident. At first, she said these men would be great but as we talked, she realized she didn't feel safe with them. "Assertive" unconsciously meant "controlling" to Ryan. "Powerful" felt "dominating." And having a clear, determined direction meant she would be left behind.

Discussions about her family revealed a mother who, she observed, was dominated by her father. "This wasn't going to happen to me," she told herself prior to puberty. The path was set. However, Ryan went too far in the safe direction. As part of her therapy, she was given an assignment to give men she normally wouldn't be attracted to more of a chance. We predicted that these men would be more outspoken, less ingratiating toward women, and significantly more forward about what they wanted. Men whose lives were going somewhere.

We agreed she would tolerate her initial reaction to them until she gained a deeper understanding of who they were. In preparation, we listed several things for her to observe and we planned to assess them jointly during her therapy.

Below is a commentary on the kind of men women can be attracted to. They grew out of Ryan's initial list and are written from a woman's perspective. I call this list The Twelve Things Women Should Avoid in Men.

1. Men Who Have Not Spent Enough Time Being Single
2. Men Who Are Little Boys Looking For Mommy
3. Men Who Are Rigid and Controlling
4. Men Who Have a Poor Work Ethic
5. Men Whose Mothers Still Dominate Their Lives
6. Men Who Do Not Want Children (*And You Do*)
7. Men Who Can't Co-parent
8. Men Who Can't Ask for What They Want Without Melting Down

9. Men You're Not Physically Attracted To
10. Men with Whom You Can't Successfully Engage in Problem-Solving
11. Men Who Tell You Feeling is Something You Do With Your Hands
12. Men You Never Feel Accepted or OK With

Here's a description of each of them.

1. Men Who Have Not Spent Enough Time Being Single

It's imperative that the man you select for your lifelong mate has invested enough time being single. This is true for both men and women for a number of reasons. But at this time, I want to focus on a man's capacity to commit.

What does being single have to do with one's ability to commit, you may ask? A lot, especially in the ability to give up the fantasy of a bachelor's lifestyle.

A man's fantasy of the bachelor's lifestyle involves an unending supply of physically gorgeous women he can date casually while having a sexual relationship. It's not that men are animals; it's more complicated than that.

Two factors predispose men to the fantasy of the bachelor's lifestyle. First, on average, men experience their sexual drive at a higher intensity than women. A study shows that men think about sex (depending on their age) anywhere from every four to eleven minutes![1] (Of course there are exceptions to this trend when a women's libido matches any man's.) Secondly, men are not socialized to express as wide a range of feelings as women. This renders them more dependent on sexualized forms of intimacy than other kinds.

After a series of relationships, men begin to understand and appreciate the more comprehensive agenda women have. They discover, to their continued astonishment, that having sex with multiple partners isn't even on her list of desires. The reality that the bachelor's fantasy will never happen can only be fully accepted by dating and experiencing a good number of relationships. When men can conclude that "I've been there and done that" and experience a woman as a person with hopes and dreams, then they could be ready for commitment and marriage.

Women, be careful of the man who hasn't been single long enough. He's more prone to have a mid-life crisis if he hasn't fully reality-tested his bachelor's fantasy. This was an early sign overlooked by Ryan that exacted its toll long before mid-life.

2. Men Who Are Little Boys Looking For Mommy

A certain number of powerful, accomplished women have a tendency to pick men who are little boys looking for mommy. From the outside looking in, these women are admired for their education, careers, vision, energy, purpose, and the strength of their personhood. However, inside they still doubt themselves. To ensure the power and control they've fought so hard to attain, they fall in love with the gentle teddy bear—a teddy bear who will never challenge or threaten them.

These kind of men are often created by their mothers—"the prince" raised in an environment where they wanted for nothing and were indulged at every turn. Their mothers likely had a marriage only in name with fathers who were absent or distant. These teddy bears never got to see any man relate to a woman other than through their mother's role; they expect the same treatment for the rest of their lives. Look out if they continue to have excessive involvement with their mothers. Although you may be the recipient of their generosity, you'll find they often allow others to use them. Rather than operating on the principle of give and take, they indulge everyone's expectations in a series of appeasements. (We'll discuss this more in Men Whose Mothers Still Dominate Their Lives).

The problem with these men is almost identical to challenges described for men in "Women Without Power." That is, you become bored with them as the years pass and your responsibilities grow. As your burden builds, your respect for them slides. Repeatedly, you will look at them with a clear feeling of needing help and conclude they're not strong enough to lend you any credible assistance. This realization will seep out in critical remarks that will further deteriorate their confidence and their scant ability to muster strength at the most crucial junctures. Meanwhile, your frustration will grow at a time when children and mortgages weigh in as part of the equation.

If you recognize yourself in this relationship, you need professional help. If you are unmarried but recognize your attraction to these men who want to relate to you as mommy, deal with your discomfort of being with a stronger man who can fully be your partner. In the long run, you have much more to gain by marrying your peer rather than your dependent. Ryan was already beginning to understand this lesson before entering therapy.

3. Men Who Are Rigid and Controlling

Marriage and parenting will constantly challenge everyone with the ongoing need to make changes. Growth is the euphemism we use to describe this painful process. These challenges can ultimately be rewarding but they are difficult. One of the surest ways to make this process nearly impossible is to marry a rigid and controlling man.

The rigid and controlling man is anxious and afraid, *yet he doesn't know it*. This makes life with him especially difficult. He's too afraid to construct a partnership in which the natural strengths of each partner, by virtue of their merit, has a chance of making the best contribution to the marriage. In an authoritative style and driven by his anxiety, he tightly controls the marital and family process to the detriment of everyone.

Often (but not necessarily) the rigid and controlling man cloaks himself in tradition. As part of his dedication to tradition, he expects his wife and children to practice obedience and fulfill predefined roles. He does this because he's looking for a life path without risk. And you've probably guessed it by now—the more trying times become, the more rigid and difficult he becomes at the worse possible times. This controlling man likely shows an inability to ask for what he wants without melting down (described under Men Who Can't Ask for What They Want Without Melting).

If your dating history suggests you are attracted to rigid and controlling men, you need to find out why. It can be anything from too strong of a need to feel protected, insufficient development of your own life goals, or a history of childhood abuse. Time spent in therapy with a psychologist would be well spent before you marry this man.

4. Men Who Have A Poor Work Ethic

Men who have a poor work ethic and men who are little boys looking for mommy likely go hand and hand. In either instance, you need to be careful before you sign up for a life of heavy responsibility with little support. If he also rings the bell for men whose mothers still dominate their lives (see Men Whose Mothers Still Dominate Their Lives), you have what I call the *teddy bear triad*.

The man who fits the teddy bear triad initially shows up as soft and cuddly. He's not a threat to you. He can be warm and ingratiating, a skill he honed with his mother who rewarded compliance with her agenda and thus controlled him. Most women are not attracted to this man without real power and thus successfully avoid his charms. If you are attracted to this guy and marry him, he'll frustrate you before your fifth year of marriage, guaranteed. Ryan's ex-husband fit the teddy bear triad.

5. Men Whose Mothers Still Dominate Their Lives

The final leg of the *teddy bear triad* is unique and easily identifiable. It will rear its telltale signs around holidays, birthdays, and family gatherings. It will even show up in his apartment. His mother will continue to expect involvement in his life. If he should decline or modify her wishes, she will react with anger and invoke guilt. He will do everything possible to avoid feelings of guilt and will juggle your wishes along with his mother's in an attempt to appease the two most important women in his life. What's missing in this dance when the music never stops is what *he* wants. Without this vital source of inner connection, nothing he agrees to is sustainable or consistent. He will drift into any number of commitments that will ultimately polarize you as the evil witch. This role will be assigned to you by his mother and ratified by other family members.

6. Men Who Do Not Want Children (And You Do)

It's frightening how often women marry a man who expresses doubt about wanting children. But what's a woman to do? A very large proportion of men feel ambiguous about having children and only discover after the fact that it's worth it. Thus, the strategy of taking *one step at a time* works more often than not. It's indeed wise not to scare away a guy you love by introducing this blockbuster issue too early.

This said, still be cautious about this strategy. If a guy is adamant around not wanting children and you marry him with the hope that you can change his mind, you're taking a big risk. Moreover, I have found that these men's commitment to parenting isn't all that strong, which means you'll have the opportunity to be superwoman by taking on tasks you'll have to accomplish alone. Early on in the relationship, casually ask him how he feels about children. Be careful of men whose childhood was troubled or chaotic; they seem most hesitant about having children of their own.

7. Men Who Can't Co-Parent

There is a difference between men who *won't* co-parent and men who *can't* co-parent. If they won't co-parent, they either didn't want children in the first place or they are stuck in a time warp five decades old. If they can't co-parent yet agreed to have children, you and your unborn are in major trouble.

Men (or women) who can't co-parent should never have children. Their capacity to love children is limited; they frequently lack tolerance; they don't want to make the necessary investment and sacrifice. At best, they'll be an absent parent and model for your children how *not* to build a marriage. The worst almost has no limit; let it be said they'll be hostile and angry.

To screen out the man who can't co-parent, volunteer to baby sit children with your significant other to see how he reacts. If possible, take the kids for a ride in his car or, better yet, take them to his condo. If he stresses out over a child acting like a child, and seems to overlook the joy of caring for a little one, you may have a man who can't co-parent.

8. Men Who Can't Ask For What They Want Without Melting Down

The vulnerability we feel in intimate relationships causes us to be hypersensitive. It's why we can fight over the most inane issues, such as failing to pick up one's socks, neglecting to put the cap on the toothpaste tube, forgetting something at the grocery store, arriving later than planned, omitting a phone call, not providing the right

There's an unspoken expectation of perfect responsiveness in every intimate relationship.

look, the right response, the right touch. Anyone in a relationship for longer than one year could add to this list of seeming atrocities.

Why are we are so sensitive to disappointment in our intimate relationships? How do we better tolerate the slights and indignities and outright abuse in almost every other relationship?

It's because there's an unspoken expectation of perfect responsiveness in every intimate relationship. This expectation, inevitably doomed for disappointment, causes many relationships to become painful battlegrounds. Behind this expectation is the fantasy of a perfect love (discussed in "Romantic Ideals that Hurt"). It's an expectation well beyond what any real person could possibly meet. Coming to terms with this discrepancy—that is, the wish for perfect responsiveness and the reality that no one has the perfect spouse—is critical to the long-term stability and viability of any marriage.

A man who can't ask for what he wants without melting down hasn't accepted that love isn't perfect. Many issues that could be resolved through communication and cooperation will unnecessarily ignite quarrels and chaos. These men frequently cannot problem-solve with you (see Men with Whom You Can't Successfully Engage in Problem-Solving). If they are also rigid and controlling (see Men Who Are Rigid and Controlling) and have little or no ability to express feelings (see Men Who Tell You Feeling is Something You Do With Your Hands), then you're voluntarily signing up for decades of problems with an angry and verbally abusive guy.

9. Men You're Not Physically Attracted To

This is rarely a problem for men, but sometimes a problem for women. It's important to be physically attracted to the man you're thinking of marrying. It's not enough that he's taller than you and provides well. You'll have to sexualize this relationship throughout the years and physical attraction plays an important role. Although attractiveness may not seem as important to you in the beginning, it helps sustain the necessary passion and connection. In time, it will prove more important to you and especially to your future husband. If he becomes conscious of your lukewarm connection, then trouble lies ahead. Either way, both of you lose the chance to relate in a way successfully married couples do.

10. Men You Cannot Successfully Engage in Problem-Solving

It's hard to find a more important couple skill than problem-solving. On the surface, it seems like it should be relatively easy, but it isn't. Too many people don't even know what they want when they enter a problem-solving discussion. They begin with angry feelings and expect their mates to comb through it and help them figure out what they want. Expecting the issue to be self-evident is usually lost in a frequent blizzard of anger and put-downs.

The initial rule in problem-solving is this: If you can't answer the question "*what do I want,*" then you're not ready to begin a discussion. It's time to bite your tongue and say nothing until you know.

Other important rules for problem-solving are:
- He can ask for what he wants but is he able to accept 'no.'
- He attempts to find consensus but realizes it isn't always possible. Sometimes plain old horse-trading is necessary (e.g., "Okay, I'll go to your nephew's birthday party if you'll trade me a baseball game.").
- He raises only one issue at a time.
- He's appreciative and content when given something.
- He accepts that every problem is not immediately solvable and you can agree to disagree.

Of course, these rules apply to you as well. In my experience, a couple who can produce an agreement in one out of every four problem-solving attempts is going to be okay! What destroys a relationship is the hopelessness of traversing the same old ground with no solution in sight. I suggest you avoid the guy who cannot problem-solve.

11. Men Who Tell You "Feeling" is Something You Do With Your Hands

How much do I need to say about this? If you're actually attracted to this guy—and plenty of women are—get into therapy now. Look past any semblance of strength or accomplishment and see how immature and underdeveloped these men are. Typically, they have an authoritarian style and dismiss sentimentality. However, they could evidence the *teddy bear triad*. To a greater degree than others, these concrete-thinking men enter occupations that heavily rely on logic (e.g., engineering and computer programming).

12. Men You Never Feel Accepted or OK With

Ask yourself this simple question, "How do I feel about myself when I'm around him?" If you don't feel occasionally loved, almost always accepted and affirmed, appreciated, admired, comfortable and relaxed, there's a problem.

For the sake of discussion, I'm assuming you like who you are and the problem is with him (although some women don't like who they are and neither do their partners.) If you're in a situation in which you never feel loved and accepted, ask a girlfriend who has seen you with him to comment. It's usually fairly easy for others to see if there's acceptance. You need to feel accepted and OK with the man you love.

Ryan's Story

Ryan eventually fell in love with a guy who was both sensitive and powerful. She married a business executive a year after she finished her therapy. He was career-focused; he could tell her no when he didn't want to do something; he enjoyed sports, cars, and water rafting. She felt safe with him even though he was more powerful

than what she'd been accustomed to. Ryan finally had the true partner she always wanted—someone who could give as much as she
could. I knew Ryan would be fine when she began to see the little
boy still existing behind the facade of accomplishments and power.
She found a better way of being safe than marrying a man who
hadn't matured.

[1] Shanor, Karen. *The Shanor Study: The Sexual Sensitivity of the American Male.*
New York, Dial Press. 1978. p. 103

Some people don't know where to point themselves.

JF, A PATIENT (1998)

⊂◯⌯⊃

21

Twelve Things Men Should Avoid in Women

erry's marriage ended on a battle-fatigued field of frustration. He spent 26 years trying to extinguish his wife's smoldering resentment. These feelings rarely flared into a combative inferno but appeared in day-to-day interactions that should have been simple. She was never content. When it was his turn to make a choice, he again was getting his way. When it was her turn, the selection was tainted with a feeling that it was too little to late. When he attempted to express his concern for her happiness, she stubbornly held on to her dissatisfaction as if it was a life raft floating on a boiling sea. For years, Gerry lived with a feeling that he was responsible for her discontent. It ended when she walked out—certain of her reason and taking one half of their assets.

A couple of years passed before Gerry ventured out to date. Decades had ticked by since he was single or had sought the companionship of a woman. Now, these initial tentative steps grew into a steady stream of dinners after reviewing profiles of women at various cyber-dating sites that connect people today.

In our discussion about the ladies he was meeting, we began to identify a pattern in the behavior of the women Gerry found attractive. They all tended to become unnecessarily angry in response to minor problems. Furthermore, he was turned off by women who revealed an initial desire stronger than his. The warm, generous sweetheart wasn't attractive; the clingy, excessively dependent woman didn't stand a chance. If any of the women were prone to anger and demanding, Gerry seemed to find them, although he swore he wasn't looking for this type of companion.

Similar to Ryan in the preceding chapter, Gerry had to consciously give the woman who was generous and warm an honest chance. He had to push by his initial negative, or more accurately, a subtle feeling of indifference toward this more loving type of woman. He had to move beyond this *Purgatory of Hope* that Gina struggled with in an abusive relationship.

Our talks about his family relations in which neither his critical dad nor mom had much to give helped us understand the unconscious underpinnings of Gerry's attraction. These angry and discontent women offered him a chance to receive love in the style he was raised on. They would provide him with an opportunity to finally gain approval from someone—a person as critical and withdrawn as his parents—where it would really mean something. His parent's love was very different than someone who would give it more freely. Receiving this person's love just didn't mean as much because it didn't offer the opportunity to finish his unconscious need to be loved by his parents. Gerry wasn't picking a partner to marry as much as he was seeking someone to heal childhood wounds. Of course, this unconscious process never brought about these results; it just created more turmoil and pain.

A list of traits Gerry was assigned to look for and avoid in women was created soon after the list in the previous chapter, "The Twelve Things Women Should Avoid in Men." I've created a second list,

The Twelve Things Men Should Avoid in Women, which has been expanded from Gerry's initial items by stories and lessons from other men.

1. Women Who Rely Too Much on Physical Beauty
2. Women Without Power
3. Women Who Will Not Stand Up to Their Parents
4. Women Who Engage in Duty Sex
5. Women Who Are Too Materialistic
6. Women Whose Desire for Sex Does Not Match Yours
7. Women Whose Wish for Children Does Not Match Yours
8. Women Who Share Few Interests of Yours
9. Women You Never Feel Accepted or OK With
10. Women Who Are All Too Willing to Mother You
11. Women Who Cannot Be Vulnerable
12. Women Without Dreams

1. Women Who Rely Too Much on Physical Beauty

Most men are practically helpless when they have the chance to date a woman with a pretty face. Her beautiful body and/or face suspends the average man's ability to look beyond the packaging and discern for himself if this person is someone to build a relationship with. The powerful physical experience men have during sexual attraction must be controlled if they are to objectively evaluate the person they're getting involved with. The question they need to ask themselves is: "This is nice, but who are you?" If they have the courage to ask themselves this tough question often and early in the relationship, the answer becomes clear.

To get this clarity, it could mean fighting off feelings of doubt and insecurity. These insecurities could include thoughts like *I won't find another woman to love. This may be my last chance. Maybe I am being too critical.* Ignoring these feelings could cause a man to settle for someone who isn't just right for him. This question needs serious consideration before the obligation builds and the relationship takes on a momentum of its own. The goal is to peer into the future knowing that down the road, you'll know much more about the person you are with. If you don't realize that the physical beauty will mean a whole lot less than it does now, you're not ready for a long-term commitment.

Don't underestimate the power of physical beauty. This relationship will not be your last opportunity to enjoy it. Be careful of women who are gorgeous and especially those who excessively rely on this strength to attract men. Repeatedly ask yourself, "Who is she?"

2. Women Without Power

Interpersonal power is the ability to influence. A woman must be able to alter her relationship with her parents from being a child to that of an adult; to earn the respect of her friends; to be seen as competent and valuable by her coworkers; or to do all of these with the man she loves. Interpersonal power requires the courage to be assertive when needed and appropriate.

Many men are attracted to the softness of passive women. Let's admit it, traditional women don't challenge the notion of being a man and are initially very easy to be with. It's very comfortable to slide into accustomed roles handed down through the eons of time and resilient mores of our culture. As if this wasn't enough, there's something about this softness that arouses the role of protector within men—a familiarity that readily allows men to feel like men. This is much more comfortable than to remain open to examining the roles we unconsciously adopt. We aren't questioning fairness in behavior or stifling a need for recognition and mutuality. In short, men relax with these women.

The problem with these women is that you'll become bored as the years pass and your responsibilities grow. As your burden builds, your respect for them slides. At some level, you'll look at her with a vague feeling of needing help and conclude that she's not strong enough to lend you credible assistance. This realization will come out in a variety of critical remarks that will further deteriorate her confidence and her scant ability to help you. Meanwhile, your vulnerability to an affair will grow at a time when children and a mortgage weigh in as part of the equation. If you recognize yourself already in this relationship, you need professional help. If you are unmarried but recognize your attraction to these women without power, deal with your discomfort of being with women who can fully be your partner. In the long run, you have much more to gain by marrying your peer rather than your dependent.

3. Women Who Will Not Stand Up to Their Parents

As you would expect, women without power and women who will not stand up to their parents tend to go hand-and-hand. These women prove to be too weak to support you when you most need it. The fact that they haven't learned to set limits with their parents signals major unresolved issues that will be a source of irritation throughout any marriage.

These women are caught between roles. On the one hand, they're fighting for their independence and trying to establish their personal meaning for life. On the other hand, they're playing the role of the obedient and subservient child while partially enjoying their protected child role. If you marry this woman, you will feel like a parent coping with an adolescent in years of teenage rebellion.

Why? Because she hasn't fully separated from her parents and hasn't declared her independence either to them or herself. Consequently, an opportunity for cooperation will feel to her like acquiescence. Let me say that again. Any opportunity you might provide for cooperation she will interpret as acquiescence and frequently reject.

These women come with an ever-present need to rebel. Imagine how this will affect your relationship. They will repeatedly raise the contrarian view—you might say the sky is blue and they will point out

190 | If These Walls Could Talk

its white clouds. A thousand times they will bounce off of anything you say, driven by a fear that they're being swallowed up and are losing their identity. You'll lose countless opportunities and precious moments to affirm your point of view and join together on obvious areas of agreement. In time, this pattern becomes a predictable source of irritation and frustration. The more you press your point of view hoping to find some validation, the more her anxiety will rise up to set the stage for more of the same.

The powerful guy with a need to take care of emotionally immature women frequently finds himself locked into these relationships. Like anyone involved with women without power, you need to look at your discomfort with powerful women. You also need to ask yourself how do you really feel in the presence of a woman who is her own person, who has fully separated from her family of origin.

If you struggle with her for every morsel of consensus, then look to see if she has done the necessary work to wrestle her identity from her parents and claim her adulthood.

4. Women Who Engage in Duty Sex

The vast majority of women consent to sex out of a sense of obligation to some degree. Often they don't want to have sex but do anyway, knowing that as they warm up, it becomes an intimate and enjoyable experience. This is OK to some degree and men need to accept this, especially in light of what we will discuss in Women Whose Desire for Sex Doesn't Match Yours. They're being generous at these times because they care about you and want to meet your needs. It's OK to accept the slow start; listen to their requests about foreplay and kindness to gently ease into sex.

However, you do want to avoid the woman who engages in too much duty sex. If you get involved, you'll feel rejected by this woman for years in an important area, as Gerry did. What do you look for? Look for the woman who initiates sex, at least occasionally. This indicates she has her own well-developed libido and will bring something to your sexual relationship greater than compliance and duty.

5. Women Who Are Too Materialistic

Most women have high on their "criteria" list a partner who can help them build home and hearth. They want a good provider, which is consistent with their desire to raise a family. Obviously, this is a constructive use of a couple's resources and benefits society as a whole. Women sometimes help to remind us of this priority. However, some women put too much emphasis on loving a rich man and living a lifestyle they deem essential and foremost. This lifestyle is a world of the *finest things* that can only be bought.

I've heard of a private night class in San Diego that purports to teach how to marry a millionaire. Instructors will tell you where these "*successful*" (notice how we automatically assume success means money) men congregate, the interests they have, the behaviors of a woman who would attract them and more. The assumption is that having money correlates with contentment when in reality it offers nothing of the sort. Lots of money can contribute to financial security, provided you live within your means. It can free you to pursue more worthwhile opportunities, assuming you'd recognize them and had the self-discipline not to let your life slip into the abyss of profane consumption and social-class isolation.

Men already experience an inordinate amount of pressure to succeed financially. Becoming involved with a woman with excessive desires for materialism will exacerbate this pressure and prevent the couple from focusing on what's fulfilling in their lives. Financial security is fine, providing you know the costs it exacts on you to achieve it. Most men never evaluate this cost. The fortunate ones make a midlife correction as their financial security builds and they sense the limits of the tool we call money. The unfortunate men continue to hone their ability to acquire more stuff that they'll never use to build a life worth living. If they're not extremely careful, this financial resource will saddle their children's ability to develop self-discipline and purpose. We live in a consumer-oriented society that does not fully appreciate the limits of money. We're still dazzled by it beyond what it can really help us do. Its value is still way over the top as evidenced by the fascination with the rich and famous. Be careful of the woman who is fascinated with glamour and *success*.

6. Women Whose Desire For Sex Doesn't Match Yours

On average, women are unlikely to ever want as much sexual contact as men. Of course there are exceptions; a woman can be more sexual than her male partner. But by and large, men frequently feel there isn't enough sexual activity in their relationships. This fact was poignantly revealed in a Dear Ann Landers column[1] several years ago when a disturbingly large number, 70% of women, admitted they could go without sexual intercourse providing they had enough hugging, cuddling, and communication! This doesn't bode well for marriage in general and becomes the bed upon which seeds of discontent are sowed, where men drift away with vague feelings of rejection.

We're not that far from a time and place when Puritan and Victorian ethics suppressed women and any expression of their sexuality. Although significant progress was made during the twentieth century, thousands of years of cultural indoctrination have not been fully undone. However, some women are further along in nurturing their sexuality than others. Given how important sexual intimacy is to most men, it's wise to pick one of these more developed women.

A confident thirty-year-old single male said to me in session, *I want to meet a woman who wants to go to Mardi Gras and yank up her shirt.* This was a guy unafraid of a woman who understood the power of her sexuality and had the courage to use it. To him, this woman would be adventuresome, creative, and playful. She'd make the commitment of fidelity not seem so dreary or burdensome. This woman could feel her own lust and required her desire to be satisfied. This woman would be open to new ideas and experiences that keep the intimacy alive. Although public displays of nudity are not the criteria for an adventuresome mate, look for signs of playfulness and sexual comfort.

Nice girls are often very safe girls, but don't choose them to the exclusion of a woman with a strong sexual identity. It's a troubling sign if she only wants to undress in the dark, is reluctant or embarrassed to be seen naked, or has feelings of guilt associated with her sexual behaviors. Make sure the woman you choose has a strong and secure sense of her sexual identity that won't atrophy into the duty sex performed by too many married women as another chore.

7. Women Whose Wish for Children Doesn't Match Yours

If you do want children and the woman you love doesn't, you're in trouble. It's more likely you don't want children and she does. The formula still amounts to trouble. As her biological clock ticks its relentless countdown toward infertility, she'll begin to press for children or become resentful that you refuse. It's imperative that you raise the issue of children with the woman you have just begun to love and listen carefully. Many women camouflage this issue, not wanting to scare off a man who just might turn out to be a great provider, companion, and father. That's why you have to listen carefully. If you're sure you don't want children and she does, then you have problems. Or perhaps you want two children and she wants five and she wants to stay home as a full-time mother. That's a problem, too.

A word to those convinced they don't want children. Although I wasn't totally closed to the idea of having children, I was perfectly content to live my life with my wife, family, friends, and career without children. I was apprehensive about the changes entailed with bringing another life into my world. I wasn't sure if I'd feel that it was worthwhile and if I could sustain the effort needed to raise a child for two decades. In discussing this agonizing decision with friends, I'd joke about how *it's the one decision in life that you can't get out of.* My wife would seek to reassure me with... "don't you think you're underestimating the love you'll get out of the relationship with your child?"

Her words meant very little until the day my first daughter was born. The love I felt for her was instantaneous at birth—and overwhelming. I repeatedly marveled at how I underestimated the joys of parenting and just how much it changes one's house into a home. I could have missed one of the most important roles in my life had it not been for the gentle persistence of my wife wanting children.

Nevertheless, if you're completely sure you don't want children, don't marry a woman who wants to be a mother.

8. Women Who Share Few Interests of Yours

If playing and watching sports, building your career, tackling home improvement projects and hanging out with your friends is what you enjoy now, it's likely you'll continue to enjoy them after you get married. Think of the conflict that will be generated for any couple whose interests are not shared. Contrast this with a couple who have shared interests in tennis or golf or other sports. These can be very positive points of connection as the years pass.

Similarly, determine if your prospective partner will share your patterns involving finances, home decoration, interests in current events, politics, reading, movies, music, and friends. A prospective spouse doesn't have to be a perfect match in all these categories. However, I'd advise that the woman you pick to be your lifelong mate share a minimal of one out of every three of your interests to ensure a viable relationship for the long term. This may a modest number but the third that she does share has to be real. That is, if she's just tolerating attending the baseball games you love, this doesn't count toward the necessary one third. If she reads the sports page after you, then her interest is legitimate and you have something to genuinely share.

9. Women You Never Feel Accepted or OK With

Some people are attracted to and are driven by negative reinforcement. These men (or women) are not attracted to partners who are generous with their love and acceptance. I have found that when they examine how they feel, they are actually turned off by warm, positive overtures. They tend to experience them as insincere or even pathetic! To them, approval and acceptance feels the sweetest when (rarely) given by a person who primarily is critical, cool, and nonaccepting.

The result is a tendency to connect with women who fuel your feelings of insecurity and self-doubt. You'll spend years trying to please this partner who will only occasionally support you with a morsel of approval. As the years pass, this partner will respect you less and less while your exhaustion builds and your ability to please her becomes less and less. This was Gerry's experience.

If your dating or marital history suggests a pattern of attraction to this type of partner, invest in professional consultation. If you are already married to her, you need individual and marital therapy in that order. You and your counselor will need to understand why you can't accept love that's freely given. There is a reason... one you're probably not going to like, but will find valuable over time. A word of caution. If you are quick to anger and you discover that your spouse is withholding and unavailable, resist the impulse to blame her. The cause is fear, not malicious intent. Give your spouse a chance to grow with you. If she refuses, then move on without her.

> *Traditional women don't challenge*
> *the notion of being a man and are*
> *initially very easy to be with.*

10. Women Who Are All Too Willing to Mother You

Some men look to marry women who will mother them. This is frequently confused with a woman's ability to *nurture* them. They won't be disappointed in their search for these women, for many will eagerly volunteer to fulfill this desire. In the long run, however, these men become depressed and their future wives are often angry. How could this quid-pro-quo possibly turn so negative as time goes on? One only needs to look at the reasons this couple came together. It is here we find the sources of attraction for this couple who so adroitly do the steps in a dance others readily recognize.

The woman who volunteers to mother you looks for two primary things. The first is a high need for control. These women can be identified by a demeanor that is overtly strong, who have very definite ideas and taste, and who tend to get their own way. It is their tendency to get their own way that negates the value of the previous two attributes. Nevertheless, they can't imagine depending on others. The idea of sharing decision making seems foolhardy and an unlikely proposition. And in time, they help create men who are truly inept.

The second reason why these women volunteer to mother their men has to do with their fear of becoming involved in any relationship that would open normal levels of vulnerability. Their discomfort with their own vulnerability can even include a feeling of dislike for this part of themselves. Long before your relationship began, they decided that they were unlovable when vulnerable—if it was momentary or otherwise appropriate. They select men who are unlikely to reach this part of themselves. In time, however, they resent these men who fuel their anger and disparagement. This often gives rise to her husband's depression.

If you're single and your pattern of dating shows a tendency to get involved with women who want to mother you, you're not ready to get married. Find a psychologist to work with and find why you look at women with an eye toward what they can do for you and why you're so afraid to form adult attachments. This isn't rocket science but missing this call can explode in your face.

11. Women Who Cannot Be Vulnerable

As mentioned above, this woman may appear as someone who wants to mother you, but not necessarily. She may be feminine in dress and in many aspects of behavior in the roles that she plays. However, this woman rarely cries or is willing to engage with you in a heartfelt conversation. Like the mothering woman above, they have an underlying fear of becoming involved in any relationship that would open up even normal levels of vulnerability. Because they're afraid to get close, they'll show up with a diminished capacity to participate emotionally and sexually in the relationship.

12. Women Without A Dream

If a woman's primary purpose in life is to marry, stay home, and have babies, be careful. This goal in life needs to be distinguished from the woman who has completed her college education, has begun a career, has lived on her own, and then decides—in conjunction with her husband—to stay home and raise their children. The sequence doesn't have to be career first and then family; it can be family first and career later. But she does need to be her own person. The distinction is between a woman who has not risked being independent versus one who has emerged from this developmental challenge of adulthood. The woman without a dream has not fully grown up; she isn't her own person and doesn't really make choices. Rather, she's playing a culturally prescribed role. In time, she will find you controlling and will perhaps resent the function she allowed herself to drift into. If you're attracted to these women, you're likely also attracted to Women Without Power. The risk is you'll feel bored and burdened.

Gerry's Story

Gerry is still in therapy and dating. He has yet to find anyone to settle down with although he may have prematurely let go of a couple of relationships that had real promise. The time he has invested in dating has been worthwhile. Gerry has become conscious of his tendencies and I believe he'll avoid marrying a woman who is angry and unsupportive.

---

[1] c.f. Farrell, Warren, 1988, pg. 195

Love and religion are the two most volcanic emotions to
which the human organism is liable, and it is not surprising
that, when there is a disturbance in one of these spheres,
the vibrations should readily extend to the other.

HAVELOCK ELLIS, 1936

22

Before You Get Married

Monsignor Davis's big-hearted, accepting presence could get lost through the telephone. That low, strong voice, worthy of the cavernous cathedral it had to fill on Sunday mornings, intimidated anyone who wasn't familiar with the man.

Monsignor called and said, "Dr. Habib, I'd like you to do a premarital session with a couple, Nick and Heather."

"Sure Monsignor. What's your concern?" I asked.

"They're pretty young," he responded.

"How young?" I asked with more than a hint of exasperation he'd understand.

"Nick is 19 and Heather is 18," Monsignor stated firmly.

"Do they *have* to get married?" I speculated.

"No. No, it's nothing like that. I think you should meet with them."

"Why, Monsignor, you know I never recommend marriage for anyone under 25 years of age."

"I know," Monsignor said, undeterred. He still wanted me to do this premarital consult and I agreed.

The day arrived for Nick and Heather's relationship evaluation. I'd already loaded the cassette recorder with a blank 90-minute tape they would take with them. When I first saw them sitting together in the waiting room, they looked every bit their age. They had in hand the completed personality tests I requested. I had to remind myself to suspend my skepticism so this next 90 minutes wouldn't be a hollow exercise.

Nick was a sophomore in college and Heather was a freshman. He wanted to be an architect and Heather listed a few career possibilities while concluding there wasn't any rush. They both held part-time jobs and planned to finish their education.

Example of Problem-Solving

"Can you give me an example of a problem you had recently in your relationship and how the two of you worked it out?" I asked.

Heather and Nick looked at each other. Heather responded, "My parents wanted to pick the restaurant for the rehearsal dinner and I agreed with their choice before checking it out with Nick." Nick just smiled, which invoked a sheepish look on Heather's face.

"So what happened next, Nick?" I asked.

"I said I wanted to pick the restaurant because my family and I were paying for it. Also, Heather and her mother have been picking almost everything else," Nick said without anger.

"So I went to my mother," Heather followed, "and told her we were having second thoughts about where to hold the rehearsal dinner."

Nick added, "I asked her to say 'we' so that I didn't look like the bad guy." Heather nodded her head with understanding.

I was impressed so far. It was clear they handled this issue with unusual skill and maturity. Heather immediately owned her mistake. Nick knew what he wanted and just asked for it. Heather didn't allow herself to be pulled between her family and Nick. She clearly backed him. Neither allowed the strong emotions involved to interfere with their ability to problem-solve. I sensed that Heather didn't avoid conflict, given how she initiated the discussion. (I would check this again later to be sure.)

Feel Like You're Missing Something?

"Have you considered that you might feel like you missed something 10 or 15 years from now if you marry right away?" I asked later in the interview.

"Sure, but doesn't everyone have those feelings?" Nick asked me. "I expect I'll always have some attraction to other women or other what-might-have-beens," he said.

"What about you, Heather? Are you sure you don't want to graduate from college first and get your career started?" I asked.

"I am going to do that anyway. But I know you're asking if that sounds like a good thing to do while being single," she stated.

"Yes, Heather, that's what I am asking."

"Well, it does sound good," she stated while glancing at Nick. He playfully frowned. "But marrying Nick now sounds better immediately," she said, watching Nick's frown transform into a thankful smile.

We continued to discuss several issues, many of them listed below. My reluctance to recommend marriage persisted, although I had to remind myself of their young age after watching their relationship unfold.

"Do you think our relationship is strong?" Nick asked, piquing Heather's interest. "I mean, aren't we good together? We love each other and to give this up just to get more experience isn't something either one of us wants to do." Heather nodded in agreement.

"So you'll remember that you jointly made a choice, which always means to exclude other possibilities, and will not blame the other for giving up your chance to date during your young adult years?" I asked once more. They looked at each other and without words agreed.

I had to admit to them *and* to myself that they were indeed good together. To say they were mature beyond their years wasn't enough. Before and after seeing Nick and Heather, I have met with many couples younger than 25 and I felt the vast majority would end up in divorce or a painful coexistence. Nick and Heather were that rare exception. Both could take ownership and control powerful feelings while staying connected to what they wanted. Both could be appropriately transparent. Neither was using their relationship as a refuge from their individual growth. Despite all these strengths, though, I was still hesitant to recommend marriage given the changes this relationship would have to undergo in the next seven to ten years.

The Premarital Blueprint

Nick and Heather had a premarital blueprint. This blueprint attempts to predict strengths and weaknesses in a couple's relationship to help avert despair and exhaustion that might be entailed in identifying the reoccurring themes in their marriage.

The premarital blueprint likely includes a personality test, a single 90-minute recorded interview, and the option of a written report. The audiotape is for them to review later and reflect on it. At the end of the interview, they're asked to make an appointment five years from now to see how they are doing.

A good premarital blueprint should attempt to predict the relational terrain that lies ahead. This helps minimize the despair, futility, and frustration that accumulate after amassing seven to ten years of experience. This is what destroys marriages. To minimize these feelings, the psychologist might predict, for example, that a relationship has a traditional power balance (husband has primary influence). It follows, therefore, that in time the wife might feel resentful and withdraw sexually. The husband might feel the burden of responsibility and lose respect for the woman he loves today.

It's important that the blueprint states this possibility beforehand, providing some sense of control and predictability. In this example, they know that a partnership-oriented balance of power needs to be developed. Feelings of hope are preserved for the couple when the possible changes have been anticipated. The relationship has been blueprinted.

Despite their youthful ages, Nick and Heather were much more realistic about love and marriage than other young adults I've seen. This is rarely true among first-time married couples. Their love in the early stages can be much more susceptible to the hard landing into reality that correlates with the peak divorce time.

The new couple must live with an awareness that they will know much more about their spouse seven to ten years down the road than they do now. Some of these insights and relationship changes are predictable. In "Ideals that Rob," we talked about how wonderful and powerful feelings are in a new relationship. Yet it can be destructive to wish for these feelings that were once easily felt over time. Couples need to be conscious of that. In "Minutes of Love," we learned how feelings of despair can result from being unrealistic about how much love is felt in an ongoing relationship such as marriage. The new relationship must distinguish between love and commitment and accept that love is not a constant—*commitment* is the only constant possible. We stop the search for the unattainable and accept Contentment, preferably before we say I do.

The emotional terrain needs to be blueprinted for many couples before they get married. Predicting what will likely happen in their emotional lives helps a couple navigate this course they're sure to traverse.

Future Trends

Future trends in self-improvement will include premarital blueprints—a couple contemplating marriage will sit down with a clinical psychologist (or another mental health professional who specializes in relationships) to get an objective opinion about their relationship. Is there a more life-changing decision we make in our life than whom we marry? Today we fly on the wings of hope and a prayer as we make this decision. The average couple attains more objective information when purchasing a car, house, or a financial investment than they ever acquire about the union they are forming.

The following are questions I'm asking myself to create a Premarital Blueprint.

- Is the intended union being used to find sanctuary from needed remaining individual growth of either partner?
- Where along the continuum does this couple lie... the traditional relationship and its role-defining characteristics at one end, and the true partnership at the other end?
- Does this couple's problem-solving ability produce results and consensus? My experience suggests that if one out of four discussions produces an agreement, then they achieve a passing grade!
- What were each of their parents' marriages like? This is the template upon which their own ability to be intimate was forged. It will strongly suggest the relational terrain that lies ahead.
- Are both sufficiently conscious of their inner life so that they can communicate the multitude of feelings that arise?
- Can they express powerful feelings without relying excessively on anger?

> *The average couple attains more objective information when purchasing a car, house, or a financial investment than they ever acquire before marriage.*

- How is regression handled in the relationship? (Think of regression as the enormous anger, hurt, or vulnerability we feel with our spouses. The ability to baby talk, to become sexual, playful, afraid, dependent, etc. are all examples of regression.) Are both individuals capable of it and is it reciprocal (do they take turns)?
- Do the parents, family, and friends support the marriage? Is parental involvement appropriate? Will the couple socialize with other couples?
- Has each person spent enough time being single? (To experience their individual self, apart from being in a relationship.)
- Have they made the transition from having to have another person to just wanting companionship and intimacy? Both have to know they can be alone and life can be OK. Thus intimacy is always a choice and each person has the ability to maintain appropriate boundaries during marriage.
- Do they share the same desire for children? Can they form a parenting coalition to raise them?
- Is a couple sexually compatible and sexually mature in their thoughts and behavior?
- Is there a spiritual component that this couple shares either in practice or philosophy? This component is capable of contributing essential grounding for the emotional terrain they will need to cross. I have seen very troubled marriages remain together as they work out their problems because divorce is not an option.
- How many significant relationships has each person experienced prior to meeting the other?
- Are the couples' financial expectations in line with where they are today and where the want to be in the future? Today, do they have enough income to prevent the significant burden that economic distress can impose?

- Does either person have significant psychological problems that will interfere with their ability to express or understand their own feelings and empathize with the other?

Five-Year Follow-up

Nick and Heather married regardless of my recommendation. This is usually the case although I frequently suggest they wait longer. Sometimes I recommend against marriage altogether. Monsignor Davis was as surprised as I was with the maturity of this couple, despite their age. It hasn't yet been five years since I met Nick and Heather, but I hope they return for their five-year follow up. I'm curious to know what they've built together and hope that my reservations were unwarranted.

Part 4: About Parenting and Families

...sit down before a fact as a little child, be prepared
to give up every preconceived notion.
Follow humbly wherever and to whatever abysses
nature leads, or you shall learn nothing.

THOMAS H. HUXLEY, LETTER TO CHARLES KINGSLEY, SEPT. 23, 1860

23

Bedtime for Infants and Children:
A Critical Beginning

Ken handed Maureen the warmed bottle of milk as she nestled into the padded rocking chair. It was time for bed and this was their nine-month-old daughter's last feeding. He heard his wife ask in a hushed voice to dim the living room lights and turn down the television's volume to help prepare Grace for sleep.

Ken hustled from appointed station to station, hoping to avoid another evening of crying and late-night awakenings. Often, they had to get up and bring the infant back into their bed. Anything to stop the crying. Their queen-size bed proved too small with the movements and sounds awaking both sleep-deprived parents trying to rest between Grace's awakenings.

Grace fell asleep as usual in her mother's embrace, both arms stretched above her angelic face in a position comfortable only for the very young. Getting the baby from her mom's arms to her crib without waking her was always a challenge. Success seemed more and more elusive. Ken helped his wife out of the rocking chair while clearing any obstructions on the path to the nursery. He raced ahead and clicked on the clamshell night-light, and then disentangled the crib from its toys. With strict silence in effect, communication between Ken and Maureen was via well-rehearsed lip reading, facial gestures, and hand movements.

Maureen approached the white-lacquered crib and prepared to lay Grace in it. This was the moment of truth. As she slowly slipped her right arm out from beneath her bottom, Grace stirred and softly whimpered. Maureen's left hand supported her wavy-blond hair-covered head. Then Maureen gently eased her bundle down. Both parents froze in silence, holding their breath and praying that Grace would stay asleep. They looked at each other, still ill at ease, as they exited the nursery... partially closing its door. They'd given the same strict instructions of silence to their two other children, five and seven years old, who rolled their eyes in collective annoyance. No loud laughter, talking, playing, TV, computer games, or even music. The children sighed with more than a hint of aggravation.

Just as Maureen was about to react to this perceived lack of support, Grace began crying. Both parents gave that knowing look of exasperation, which floated amid the frustration. Dad went to pick up the baby. The whole ritual had to be repeated.

Avoiding the Traps

Establishing the infant's sleeping pattern is important for the child, the parents, and everyone else in the family. For the infant, established sleeping patterns begin to build a foundation upon which the developing child is able to separate from others. It's likely a precursor to the child emerging as a confident individual, free from undue anxiety. Minimally, it denotes an evolving parent/child relationship with boundaries and room for independence. It presents a challenge for parents who no doubt care and love deeply, but who must ensure they don't react to their own anxiety.

If you are parents, perhaps you've experienced the uncomfortable feelings that go with leaving your tiny infant alone in a darkened room. The challenge entails avoiding overreacting to tearful expressions of abandonment despite an instinctual urge to soothe them. Allowing them to sleep in your bed, or sleeping or staying with them too long, is an overreaction. Our earnest desire to convey love and soothe any feelings of abandonment they might experience poses the challenge. It requires a strength to reality test just *who* is experiencing anxiety, a discipline not to sleep with them throughout the night, and a tolerance for crying. This is especially challenging.

Admittedly, the sound of a crying baby is hard to ignore. Perhaps it's genetically wired into our behavior, compelling us to heed and respond. When you're the parents who love the child, ignoring those cries can be even more difficult. Before you realize it, you're overreacting to each and every one of the child's behaviors. A pattern emerges in which excessively responsive parental behavior shapes problematic behaviors resulting in an overly stimulated child. This is at the heart of most sleeping difficulties. Let me explain.

Once they came home with the baby, they repeatedly told both older children, "Shh... the baby's sleeping." Maureen and Ken were on their way to developing a pattern of being too responsive when they first began to alter the volume of the activities within their home. Of course, in itself, this doesn't sound bad or seem unreasonable. But what followed was consistently anticipating the perceived needs of the child by making more and more elaborate adjust-

> *What began as heartfelt commitment*
> *to the perceived needs of the child*
> *evolved into Grace's expectation*
> *that someone would always be with her.*

ments. That is, the child needed to be fast asleep before they put her down. If she whimpered, the cuddling time got extended. If she cried at the onset of naps, Maureen stayed with her. If she cried at bedtime, one parent would pick her up. At times when Grace would have been content to lay or sit alone, she was held. And when she began to fuss, the devoted parents immediately jumped in.

Ken and Maureen were reacting to their own feelings about being alone. Consequently, Grace was rarely allowed to be alone. What began as heartfelt commitment to the perceived needs of the child evolved into Grace's expectation that someone would always be with her. This became her set point; she didn't feel secure in her world without the presence of others. With this overstimulation, the child had little opportunity to adjust to being alone. And when she was alone, she would panic and cry plaintively.

Grace's parents had difficulty tolerating her crying. It made them feel unnecessarily negligent. This was especially evident at bedtime because her sleep pattern still wasn't established. On average, their progress was already behind what many parents and infants had already achieved by the age of nine months.

Many parents are able to establish a pattern of sleeping through the night by the time the child begins to eat solid food. This entails two issues: 1) Setting and maintaining a consistent sleep time and 2) limiting their involvement in helping to establish sleep.

Setting a consistent sleep time helps the infant synchronize his or her internal biological clock when the rest of the family is shifting into that mode. Needless to say, this can be beneficial to the household's ambience.

Parents who limit their involvement at bedtime inadvertently avoid training their child to need a parent to go to sleep. Thus, successful parents avoid allowing the child to always fall asleep in their arms. They use a matter-of-fact tone in their voices when they leave the child's room at bedtime and during naps. This matter-of-fact tone reassures the child more than the words spoken. They can tolerate some crying. They avoid picking up the child. They rarely or never let the child sleep in their bed.

Given that, how can Maureen and Ken get Grace to establish a good sleeping pattern now that she's used to bad habits?

Establishing a Bedtime Ritual

Because Maureen and Ken were devoted parents willing to do anything for Grace's welfare, they needed reassurance that what we were about to implement was best for their baby. Both expected that Grace would get upset and weren't sure they could tolerate it.

We picked Friday night to begin the new nighttime ritual, a desirable time because neither parent had to rise for work the next day. I had Ken and Maureen imagine putting Grace in her crib at the bedtime they pick for her, covering her, and in a matter-of-fact tone say *"good-night."* This tone, which we rehearsed, is important because the child senses the parent is OK with what's happening and can often draw from this simple form of reassurance. Again, the child doesn't understand the words but derives reassurance from the absolute tone of Mom or Dad's voice.

This calming, matter-of-fact tone also helps when a parent leaves a toddler in day care or with a nanny, for example, because the child derives reassurance from it. This tone contrasts with the overly emotional one of a parent who, for example, says: "Good byeeee... mommy gonna miss you... Come give me a big kiss... I love you... ohh ... that's a big hug... let me give you one back. Bub-bye... I'll miss you ... blow me a kiss... I'll be thinking about you," etc.

This emotional tone implicitly delivers a message that something major is transpiring, not just going off to work for the day. With this approach, the parent can unintentionally raise the child's anxiety around separation. Rather than conveying love and nurturance, the parent frightens the child whenever separation is necessary. This can also be conveyed at bedtime when the child needs to be able to be OK with being alone. Thus the tone of either Ken or Maureen's voice is important when they put Grace down for bed.

Next, we talked about immediately getting out of Grace's room even though she will cry. It's OK to let her cry, I assured them. So while outside of her room, Ken and Maureen agreed to be supportive and remind each other that they're doing what's best for their daughter.

Two Types of Crying

It is important to distinguish between types of crying. Most crying is just the *plaintive type* and parents tend to become manipulated by it. That is, they overreact to it and the child learns how to solicit their inappropriate involvement by doing it.

The second type of crying is much stronger and is usually distinguished by the child's breathing pattern. Called the *distressed type*, it can be distinguished by the moments of silence as the child takes a large breath before crying out again. During this type of crying, the child seems unable to catch his or her breath. Clearly, this child needs parental soothing and attention.

Ken and Maureen agreed to limit their reaction to the plaintive crying the first night of practicing good bedtime patterns. If Grace's crying is plaintive, they should stay out of the room and allow her to cry herself to sleep. However, given the highly responsive pattern they've set up, they're likely to experience the second type of crying—distressed crying.

If Grace is crying uncontrollably, Maureen or Ken should go into the room after *ten minutes*, still talking in a matter-of-fact tone. It's OK to rub her back, cover her with her blanket, place a pacifier in her mouth, say *goodnight* in that matter-of-fact, final tone, and then get out of the room. *They should not pick her up or stay in the room more than a few minutes.* Also, they shouldn't expect Grace to stop crying before leaving the room. She won't. They're simply helping her gain control over her crying by giving her the all-important opportunity to soothe herself.

Once they're out of the room, they listen for the crying to shift from distressed crying to the plaintive form. If it does, then they stay out of the room. In time, Grace will cry herself to sleep and her parents will have made a major stride in establishing her bedtime. If she doesn't stop crying and the intensity remains that of distress, they should wait 20 to 30 minutes before going into the room and repeating the steps above.

I anticipate that Maureen and Ken will have to weather two or three re-entries into her room before they break up Grace's established pattern. After doing this the first night, the second night and subsequent naps should prove easier. During those 20 to 30 minutes between room entries, it's important that Maureen and Ken support each other by remembering they are doing what's best for their daughter.

If you have to accomplish this with your infant, note the progress you've made in converting distressed crying into plaintive crying. Implement the same pattern you did the night before. You should find your baby falls asleep faster than on the previous night. Gain strength and courage from the improvements and, remember, you're doing what's best for your child. Also, make sure any babysitters practice the same bedtime habits to prevent relapses that you'd have to endure late at night.

Sharing the Parents' Bed

In my work with parents, I've seen instances of children who are considerably older than infants still sleeping in their parent's bed. Or children who will get up in the middle of the night and climb into bed with their parents. A few parents have endorsed this sleeping pattern because of the closeness and warmth they experience.

In Orange County, California, a pediatrician named Dr. Sears encourages this practice and calls it shared sleeping (Sears, 1991). He formulated this child-rearing recommendation from the largely criticized work of Tine Thevenin (1987) who wrote *The Family Bed: An Age Old Concept in Child Rearing.*

In my opinion, this practice is not only injurious to the child but also to the marriage. Although other cultures practice these sleeping behaviors (and they may be appropriate to the child's development in that culture), in our culture, this practice consistently correlates with problems in the child and the family. For better or worse, self-reliance is highly valued and correlates with achievement in our culture.

A family struggling with this problem with older children can set similar limits and establish consistent bedtime patterns as they did with infants. They need to establish the hour of sleep consistently, and make the bedtime ritual steady and reasonable. The ritual involves getting ready for bed, discontinuing fluids at least an hour before bedtime, reading a story, then turning off the lights and leaving the child to drift off to sleep. Some parents can become manipulated into letting story time last too long. Others become hostage to falling asleep patterns that require them to lie down with the child or remain in the room until they fall asleep. Story time should last less than a half hour and parents should never have to remain until the child falls asleep.

To help the child who still requires the parent's presence to fall asleep, do the following:

1. The day of the evening that the change takes place, announce that you're making a change, tell the child his or her new bedtime and say that he/she is no longer permitted to sleep in the parents' bed. At bedtime, follow through with what you said in a matter-of-fact tone.

2. Be prepared for resistance and complaints about not being able to sleep. If the child is unable to sleep, *he/she must still lie in bed quietly*. Don't permit your child to get out of bed.

If he/she doesn't yield to your authority, you're dealing with another problem that frequently accompanies poor sleeping patterns.

3. If your child tends to join you in the middle of the night, shut your door and lock it. If you feel this inhibits your child's welfare, partially close the door and place several metal hangers or other noisemakers on the knob. This enables you to awaken and firmly insist that the child return to bed. Here, too, it's important to remain matter of fact in tone and, if need be, firm and annoyed. Your goal is to gain the child's compliance.

4. If the child cries, distinguish the types of crying as with an infant. Remember, the capacity for older children to soothe themselves is much greater than for younger ones.

5. Don't let yourself be manipulated.

6. Do expect to spend two to three nights altering the pattern.

Your assignment is to appreciate the importance of establishing bedtime patterns that promote your child's sense of well being and autonomy. It requires acknowledging and controlling your feelings for your newborn and your growing child. Your tool is to project with your voices and behaviors that the world is OK. This allows children to master the periods they are alone and lays a foundation on which confident, independent children can calm themselves.

Our lives, as we live them, are passed on to others, whether in physical or mental forms, tingeing all future lives forever. This should be enough for one who lives for truth and service to his fellow passengers on the way.

LUTHER BURBANK, (1849–1926)

24

Raising Resilient Children

"This is my egg," Adrienne declared in her three-year-old ordering of the world, "And this is your egg, Daddy, and I don't want mine broken."

"I have to break it. We're having scrambled eggs," I informed her as her face grimaced with pain for the egg as it slid from its shell into the bowl. After piercing each yolk and blending the ingredients into a now unfamiliar liquid, she still felt uncomfortable. She asked, "Which one's mine?"

The hot pan quickly congealed the mass into separable portions. I corralled a third of the steaming egg together and identified it as hers. Her world again had order.

We sat across from each other at the L-shaped breakfast bar that pushed into her armpits and wedged her into the chair. Her sweeping arms found the industrial-sized plastic ketchup bottle prompting an instantaneous desire. "I want some." She pulled the full bottle with the opened flip-top cap closer to her. Her little hands could barely palm the bottle's sides as she knocked it over in her initial attempt to pick it up. She rotated the prone container as she fumbled with it, finally managing to raise the hindquarters of the bottle.

"It's heavy, Dad," she said as she wrestled the behemoth into a more steady inverted position.

"Help me Daddy... help me," she pleaded, still persisting in a valiant attempt to get the container to relinquish some of its contents.

"You can do it, Adrienne... you can do it."

She grunted as her two fully extended arms raised the bottle while plunging the top into the scrambled eggs. Some of the eggs were pushed over the edge and fell onto the counter.

"Uhh...ERR...Uhh." I could hear as the tip came out of the eggs. Her delicate hands were on the rigid bottle's neck that resisted her pressure. "Help me, Daddy."

"You're getting it, Adrienne."

I cheered her on, although my heart wanted to reach over the inches that separated us and put an end to her struggle. She persisted with a slightly improved determination and one of her hands found the belly of the bottle. A toothpaste portion of ketchup oozed onto the eggs and an instant later, she dropped it onto the counter with a thud. The bottled squirted a similar proportion of its red content onto her nightie. Undaunted, Adrienne threw her two arms up into the air like a sprinter having just won a race and loudly proclaimed, "I DID IT... TTTT."

I held my hand out as she slapped me five with a full swing of her arm in celebration of her victory. "You did a good job. That was real hard but you did well, Adrienne," I told her with honest pride in her

There is value in allowing our children to wrestle with the hurdles they encounter.

willingness to struggle. "MOM... MOM'MM," she screamed. "I put ketchup on my eggs," she urgently wanted to share and Mom appeared, initially responding to the dubiousness of the culinary choice.

When Helping Hurts

I wasn't quite prepared for how powerful my feelings as a parent would prove to be around providing for and protecting a child. This intrinsic urge to provide—nestled inside feelings of love—generates a reflexive pattern of involvement. There are so many opportunities to interject a decision from the heart rather than occasionally allow the struggle to unfold—a decision from the head. This lesson wasn't about ketchup, obviously, but about the value of the struggle. It's about raising a child with confidence, with their individuality firmly rooted. Throughout that brief struggle (which seemed like an eternity), I wanted to reach over and help Adrienne. I had to resist this powerful impulse that came replete with nagging feelings that somehow I was neglecting her at that moment. This intrinsic need to protect and provide for our children likely has instinctual roots experienced as instantaneous and reflexive choices to take care of our young.

I've experienced similar instinctual reactions for my daughter when I'd automatically scan for skunks and raccoons in the back yard before we strolled onto the back patio on a warm summer evening. Vestiges of the hunter now in a suburban jungle, perhaps? But a parent's feelings to respond to our children's needs and protect them are strong. Only by recognizing the opportunity and the inherent value of the struggle can we give our children the chance to develop an emotional persistence and resilience (Seligman, 1996).

There is a formative value in the struggle. Let me say that again because the concept is so important in raising children. There is value in allowing our children to wrestle with the hurdles they encounter. The struggle itself builds perseverance and frustration tolerance. These ego strengths, if not impeded from developing in childhood, reverberate throughout their years in visions others would not dare to dream and in emotional resiliency to make them a reality.

Where do these opportunities to struggle and achieve occur? If you give yourself the chance to look—and can emotionally shoulder their value—they occur every day.

For infants, it's the chance to master sleeping alone and throughout the night.

For toddlers, it's the struggle to manipulate things in their world, the precariousness of mobility and the emerging acceptance of "no."

For preschoolers, it's the opportunity to weather the ups and downs of playing with other children as they struggle to learn the rudimentary "rules" of social relatedness. (Your assignment is to be especially careful as a parent not to encourage excessive dependency upon you that produces the "shy" child.)

For primary school children, it's an expectation they wrestle consistently with homework, learn the rules of communication and civility, finish chores, and cope with peer pressure.

For middle school students, it's the reasonable consequences of their behavior such as refusing to return the late library book and paying the fine.

We recognize and allow the struggle to unfold occasionally in their quiet/withdrawn times. This struggle to find autonomy strengthens in junior high children when our love has to be patient and tolerant. More and more, we allow children at this age to face the natural and available consequences of their choices and behaviors. For example, those who persistently train the parents to help them get homework started and completed may be allowed to go to school without their assignments done: a natural consequence. If there isn't one, talk to their teachers but allow them to come face to face with natural (of course, only acceptable) consequences.

For high school students, we look for every opportunity for them to make decisions. We're judicious but firm about holding the line on issues worth pursuing as a parent. Generally speaking, low priority issues are dress, clothes, hair, music, friends, and cleanliness of *their* rooms. High priority issues are school, no drugs, no alcohol, no smoking, deference/respect for authority, independence, vision, and the ability to accept responsibility. We are getting them ready to leave home as a child so they can return as responsible adults.

The Value of Struggle

The lesson here is about recognizing the formative value of the struggle. Struggling can build perseverance. For our children to develop this all-important quality, we're challenged as parents to not only act from the comfortable warmth of our hearts but from the wisdom in our heads. Self-esteem is earned, not conferred. That is, our children must walk their road alone at times to discover what they've achieved, where feelings of mastery are far more important than any single lesson. Self-esteem is the positive by-product of accepting these challenges and finding alone their ability to succeed. We cannot give them self-esteem nor undertake their challenges for them. What we *can* do is stand aside while they struggle and patiently wait, quietly believing in the inevitable opportunity to celebrate their successes.

Learn what is true in order to do what is right
Is the summing up of the whole duty of man...

THOMAS H. HUXLEY (1825–1895)

25

Neglect or Indulgence: Knowing the Difference with Your Children

*Z*achary's face turned away toward the passenger side window. "Fine" is all he mustered in response to his mother's cheerful question. She felt this conversation going nowhere. Many times, she'd traced these steps with eight-year-old Zach. It always ended with him saying little and she feeling like a failure. Now she added a nagging concern on top of her feelings of frustration. Was Zach becoming depressed? Did he feel badly about himself? Why was he so withdrawn?

Undeterred despite her frustration, she tried again.

MOM: Tell me how your day went... did you have fun? (Bright and lively without a hint of discouragement in her voice.)

ZACH: Good.

MOM: Did you play with Jamie?

ZACH: Yeah.

MOM: Talk to me... Mommy missed you today.

ZACH: It was OK.

Mrs. Green could tell Zachary was more interested in fogging the cold window with his warm breath than responding to his mom. She felt sick that her son was non-communicative and emotionally distant. She pondered if he questioned her love for him. This remote possibility kept her determined to endure any slight or hardship. She wanted to bridge the frightening, expanding rift between her son and herself.

MOM: I have a surprise for you when we get home. Do you want to know what it is?

ZACH: What.

MOM: Well... it's something you said you've wanted.

No response.

MOM: Try to guess?

No response.

When they arrived home, Mom immediately produced the gift—an action figure hero—the one she'd overheard him say "I want that" during a television commercial. Halfheartedly, Zachary opened the carefully wrapped package and took out his superhero from its plastic capsule. Five minutes later, he left the toy and both sets of wrappers strewn upon the floor.

The gift ended up on the mountain of toys in his bedroom later that evening. The large toy box overflowed beyond any chance of closing the hinged lid properly. And the smaller fraction of toys were housed in this room. The playroom warehoused a room-smothering fortune in playthings. His closest was choked with clothing.

All this and Zachary still wasn't happy. His mom became increasingly concerned with his estrangement. She was determined to try harder.

Neglect Versus Indulgence

Most parents (and some therapists) have difficulty distinguishing neglect from indulgence. In high socioeconomic homes, either material and/or emotional indulgence is the most common problem when children falter. Typically, parents in these homes are highly motivated and invested. Often this means they provide everything and anything for their children, believing that it will help them grow and flourish. Frequently, they don't get the intended results. They emotionally withdraw like Zach. Other children underachieve in academics and/or socially. Other parents become embroiled in a power struggle. All often initially assume their child isn't getting what he or she needs. They frequently but erroneously feel they've neglected their child in some way.

They're wrong on both accounts, although their hearts are in the right place. Concluding that the indulged child is neglected is a mistake and will lead parents to actually exacerbate the problem they want to relieve.

Zach is not a neglected child. On the contrary. He was suffocating from excessive availability of his mom, dad, caretakers, and the mountains of junk that crowded out his emerging sense of self. Although he's struggling and will soon complain that his parents fail to give him what he needs, he's not neglected.

Both neglect and indulgence are hurtful to the child. More than that, they produce children who are unsure about many things. Indulged children frequently suffer from high levels of anxiety whereas neglected children suffer from depression. As one would expect, both are in trouble. However, it's crucial to distinguish between neglect and indulgence if we're going to help the child as parents or as family psychologists.

Suffering from Neglect

Children suffering the effects of negligence experience depression because they frequently feel abandoned and unloved. However, the expression of these same feelings by *indulged* children must not lead us to erroneously conclude that more love and involvement is needed. Indulged children might indeed state that they *feel* unloved, but they're not unloved. Their frustration is about the parent's failure to provide for every single need in their lives.

From the child's perspective, indulgent parents implicitly promise they can provide a great deal more than they possibly can. Frustration results from a collision between the child's undeveloped initiative and the parents' failure to provide for the child's every challenge. Overinvolved parents signal their availability at every twist and turn. Whenever they fail to anticipate a need or are not available, the child feels anxiety stemming from underdeveloped independence.

Precisely because the parents attempt to thoroughly provide for the child, anxiety results. This seemingly contradictory message from the child—*I feel intruded upon/I feel abandoned*—often leaves parents feeling confused and even crazy.

Why does overinvolvement produce anxiety? It's because of the myriad of missed opportunities to *do it myself*. By missing the formative opportunities to do it themselves, indulged children develop anxiety-based behaviors like underachievement, immature social skills, avoidance, shyness, excessive dependency, and more.

Do It Themselves

Why does the usurped opportunities to "do it themselves" result in anxiety? Because it isn't just about being stubborn or emotionally unresponsive to Mom or Dad. It's about taking away opportunities to take small steps in developing feelings of mastery. Children seek a sense that they can accomplish what they set out to do. They want a can-do attitude that leads to taking worthwhile risks. They set out on adventures that lead to fulfillment. Without opportunities to succeed or fail—*to do it myself*—their capacity to cope with anxiety is frequently underdeveloped. The lifetime consequences are dramatic: chronic underachievement, co-dependency, fear of dreaming about life's possibilities, etc. Each missed opportunity puts the child further behind in his/her capability to take calculated risks and feel comfortable with people who have average boundaries and who aren't overly solicitous.

Emotionally indulged children experience people with average boundaries to be aloof, cold, and unavailable. Thus they tend to gravitate toward people, and later toward a mate, who have similar problems with independence. Initially, these relationships feel familiar and comfortable but in time, fuel anger and disrespect. Of course, indulgent, emotionally intrusive parents never intend to cause this damage. But damage is what they create.

In "Bedtime for Infants and Children," we talked about the importance of establishing an infant's bedtime and how it builds a foundation upon which the older child emerges as a confident individual. In "Raising Resilient Children," we discussed the nutritional value of struggling on one's own and how the exertion results in emotional persistence and resilience. Central to all of these lessons is an awareness on the part of the parents to control their own feelings.

Knowing When to Step Back

Parenting isn't about always promoting positive feelings. The prudent parent knows when to become involved and when to step back throughout the developmental years of their child.

Zachary is far from being unloved or neglected. To the contrary, he's an indulged child struggling for autonomy. Zachary knows that *his mom's need to talk*, to have quality time, to be included, *is stronger than his needs*. He feels his mom's needs intruding when she wants to talk in the car, when she purchases a gift, when she cuts his food, pours his milk, becomes too concerned with his dress and diet, how he expresses feelings, how he keeps his room, how he relates with his friends, siblings, relatives, even how he walks, talks, and sleeps. Zachary feels the burden of her need to be involved. Somewhere in his unconscious thoughts lurk earlier struggles for independence when she held him too much as an infant, when she became too involved with him stumbling, mealtime, bedtime and toilet-training as a toddler.

Consequently, at this time, anything Mom says, no matter how right it is, he dismisses, ignores, or defies. He's grown to anticipate overinvolvement when Mom asks the most innocuous questions. This automatic reflex can be seen in his barely discernable responsivity or when he presses his nose against the glass in the family car. Mom would have seen a much more responsive Zack moments before in his relationship with his teacher. As Zach gets older, his parents—and especially his mom—are likely to find themselves embroiled in a power struggle with him.

Zachary needs his autonomy affirmed and Mom needs to develop better boundaries. As parents, we affirm that autonomy when we actively search for ways to allow children to do things themselves, even when they struggle or show fear. This is how to demonstrate boundaries. In this situation, her problems with Zach are most overt, but her difficulties with boundaries are also found in her friendships, in other family relationships, and with her husband.

How can she mend the rift that's expanding between herself and Zachary?

Changing the Balance

Let's begin with Mom picking Zachary up from school. Mom should only say "Hello" when he climbs into the car. No bright and eager conversation. No 20 questions; no looks of concern or impatience. She needs to be perfectly willing and prepared to ride home in silence. During the silence, Mom should remember that something positive is unfolding—it's just not overt or verbal.

Specifically, Zachary is experiencing the emotional space to think and feel his own thoughts. The pressure of his mom's needs is slowly receding so that his need for interaction can emerge. When his need to talk arises, he will talk.

Remember, Zachary's problem isn't that he feels no one is available. To the contrary, Mom is so available that she is intrusive, which is easily and frequently confused. Indeed, the incidence and frequency of overinvolvement and indulgence seems to be approaching epidemic proportions among parents of the baby boom generation.

If not the second day, then by the third or fourth day, Zachary will begin to talk. At first his attempts may be piecemeal as he tests the waters. He's scared that he'll get pounced on emotionally. At some time, he will struggle with his own abilities to initiate conversation. The temptation his mom must avoid is to support his emerging early efforts by speaking for him or expounding on what he says. Mom must bite the tongue that's tied too closely to her heart and use her head rather than her heart.

This struggle is good for Zach. He might even complain about the change because part of him has become accustomed to (and reliant on) Mom's catering. She should look at this as withdrawal symptoms, but not get confused. He's grown too dependent. The fact that he might not be sure he wants to relinquish this dependence shouldn't be confused with Mom maintaining her boundaries. This is best for Zach. If Mom misreads this mixed message and indulges Zach, the process will recycle and revert to the noncommunicative pattern neither one desires. Each time it reverts back, another brick gets laid in the wall between their relationship. From this wall, Zach will wage a power struggle, beginning as early as his preteen years.

Guiding Ratio

How much should Mom talk in the car or at other times? There's an important tool here. If he produces a total of 12 words, then Mom is limited to responding with a maximum of eight. Therefore, the guiding ratio is 3:2 in word production. This is a concrete way of practicing good boundaries as parents. This same ratio applies to emotional enthusiasm that must also fall behind what Zach produces.

That is, Mom's overt enthusiasm about anything should never be greater than Zach's.

If your heart is bursting with things you wish you could share, maintain a diary that you'll give your children later. It should chronicle their lives and your experiences as a parent. The goal is to stay behind one-third of a measure. This ensures that the primary need to communicate stems from Zach's needs, not his mother's.

Similarly, she should avoid any attempt to "keep the conversation going" and, again, be totally prepared to remain silent. Silence makes some people anxious. This was true for Zach's mom (and for anyone who fills every moment with verbiage). Nevertheless, as Mom practiced decreasing how much she talked, Zachary's need to talk emerged.

Look for Reasonable Risks

Mom began to actively scan for things Zachary could undertake alone. As mentioned in "Raising Resilient Children," she was looking for reasonable risks and consequences a child at a given age can assume and thus encourage their independence. Thus, a few scrambled eggs on the counter and ketchup on her nightie is no big deal for a preschool girl. Children insisting on pouring their own milk is permitted at times. Those who want to use Scotch tape to fix their toys, sell pictures they drew, brush their teeth by themselves, walk ahead of their parents in public, or even put themselves to bed are allowed to. Boundaries are respected. The parents' need for involvement can never be consistently more urgent than the child's. This is not always easy when we love them so much and our time with them as children passes by at dizzying speed.

> *Without opportunities to succeed or fail—*
> *to do it myself—their capacity to cope with*
> *anxiety is frequently underdeveloped.*

Starting Kindergarten

When my daughter Adrienne was just shy of her fifth birthday, we started her in kindergarten. She was the youngest in her class, a liability we felt offset whatever intellectual endowment she might have acquired from two parents with Ph.D.s.

One of the first times I took her to school, I had the admittedly difficult opportunity to follow my own advice. It was especially tough because it wasn't what I had hoped for. I was looking forward to strolling with her though the school's playground, meeting some of her classmates and perhaps other parents, even saying hello to her teacher. But as we approached the gate of the school, Adrienne turned around and said, *OK, Dad, far enough.* With two outstretched arms, she physically stopped me at the fence from entering into her new world. I felt rejected and shut out. But I didn't go in. I watched my confident little girl, who for that moment looked older than 4-¾ years of age, stroll on without me. She ran up to a little friend and never looked back.

Then my feelings of pride kicked in. I wanted to support her emerging courage to go it alone, knowing what will emerge in time will be a source of satisfaction for both of us. But it was difficult. I wanted to intrude. I suspect at times I might indulge my need to be with her.

The lesson is to respect your children's boundaries throughout the years they are with you and into their adulthood. Your assignment is to recognize and control your feelings around your need for inclusion. Wait for them to come to you throughout their childhood and young adulthood. Patiently wait until they're ready to receive the love or advice you so willingly want to give.

> *The parents' need for involvement can never be consistently more urgent than the child's.*

The Transcendent: Time for Mom

Mrs. Green changed her relationship with Zach dramatically. At first she was hesitant to pull back when Zach looked like he was struggling and anxious. However, this became easier as he initiated discussions and didn't seem so withdrawn. The next thing she did was to limit the number of gifts and presents he received. This accelerated Zach's personal gains and got her to think about how she might be too available with other people as well.

Mrs. Green discovered that her struggle with Zach was just the most obvious evidence of a problem that extended throughout her relationships. The insight she gained with Zach led to profound changes in many aspects of her life. It became clear that everyone took advantage of her willingness to help, to initiate, and to be persistent. The more she did for friends and family, the less they seemed to appreciate her efforts.

The first time she said *No* to her mother's request to make last-minute changes in plans established weeks before, she noticed improvements in her mother's behavior. Suddenly her mom wasn't so sure about their relationship; for the first time in years, she seemed to realize the value it held for her. Mrs. Green noticed this change and learned how to set gentle limits when required.

In fact, there wasn't a significant relationship in her life that didn't improve because of the changes Mrs. Green had made. *You know what, it's so much easier on me now. And I am not the burden I used to be to everyone*, she said the last time I saw her. I eagerly await future discussions with her to learn of the changes good boundary-keeping has brought to her life.

What's normal isn't necessarily healthy.

WILLIAM BLAKE (1757–1827)

26

⤳⤳

Adult Children Who Hate to Visit their Parents

D o places like California, Colorado, and Florida have a greater share of adults trying to put distance between themselves and the families they live so far away from than other states?

I'm not aware of any scientific corroboration of this hypothesis. However, my observations while working and living with non-native Californians suggest this: A great many adults have yet to achieve an adult relationship with their parents.

Assuming this is true, what drove them to these distant places? Were their parents too intrusive? Did their fathers habitually demand compliance and involvement at the expense of their freedom to think and choose for themselves? Was mom an emotional burden who had to be endured throughout their childhood? Does guilt quickly surface in these people? Were family expectations so demanding that they fled from the straightjacket it imposed?

This, in fact, was Lyndsey's situation.

Lyndsey moaned each time she spoke about her trip back east for the holidays. She could already hear the same old questions and advice her parents would produce. *Haven't you found a nice boy to marry? Why don't you move closer to home? There's nothing keeping you in California.* She dreaded being asked about who she was dating, how she dressed and acted, where she tries to meet men. For her, going home was like getting a tooth extracted.

When her mom wasn't trying to probe into every corner of her life, her dad was heaping unsolicited advice on her. *How much are you paying for car insurance? Make sure you get competitive bids.* He would go on to give unwanted information on taxes, telephone service, security and personal safety devices, nutrition, religion, friends, voting preferences, home improvements, transportation, airline deals, vacations, and more.

Lyndsey didn't want any of it. Although she was 34 years old, she complained of feeling like an adolescent in their presence. When she attempted to halt this onslaught of intrusive involvement, she met head on with her mom's guilt. *I am only trying to care about you,* her mom's statements laced with anguish and hurt. Her dad reacted no less badly: *You never listen to anything.* Lyndsey was resigned to strictly surviving her visits. She always left these encounters feeling shaky and doubtful. Her therapy revealed a connection between her relationship with her parents and her fear of intimate commitment. As a result, Lyndsey feared getting involved in another relationship that threatened to dominate her life.

Becoming Friends with Adult Children

When our children reach 21 years old, our role as parents can finally shift from that of guardian to one of friendship. Although this may appear obvious, how we interact with our adult children needs to undergo a distinct and fundamental change during this time. This change is crucial if we want to have a full relationship with our children when they reach adulthood; relationships where their visits and interactions are not only motivated by a sense of duty and commitment, but a sincere desire to visit us.

I've heard many adult children who describe most, if not all, of the time they're getting ready to spend with their parents with reluctance and negative anticipation. They visit their parents only when they feel motivated by a sense of obligation resting on feelings of guilt. Years go by and nothing changes as their parents age. The chance to improve their relationship threatens to disappear. In many instances, I suspect their parents feel their children's ambivalence.

Implicit Relationship Rules

So why do some offspring dread visits with their parents while others look forward to them? Often, those who dread these visitations have parents who haven't updated a crucial dynamic in their relationship with their adult children. Let's consider some of the implicit rules in your relationship with your best friend.

Think of how you are and how you behave in a relationship with a close friend. For example, your good friend Mary was discussing a recent marital conflict with her husband. You got the impression gleaned from years of observation that he was, indeed, emotionally abusive. Would you just blurt out this interpretation? Would you take the liberty of imposing your analysis regardless of her current capacity, readiness, or willingness to cope with such information? Or would you be considerate and say much less than you would to your adult child?

> *We are much more careful, and yes, sensitive to our friend's emotional world than we seem to be with our adult children.*

If your other friend Angela was talking about her third grade son who was kept after school for misbehavior, would you draw a correlation to how she and the boy's father have allowed him to get away with murder since he began to crawl? Or would you wisely hesitate and look for an appropriate moment such as your friend's request for help in searching for answers? Most would observe the social rule that says *be careful of giving unsolicited advice.*

Often we are much more careful, and yes, sensitive to our friend's emotional world than we seem to be with our adult children. The fact that they are *your* children or that you sincerely care for them doesn't constitute a license to trample on basic rules of adult relationships. We wait until we are asked for advice by our friends. We use gentle probes that are an invitation that can be accepted or declined. We read body language that says "tell me more" or "I'm feeling overwhelmed or emotionally flooded and I don't want to talk about it." We humble ourselves (to avoid appearing superior) by mentioning our similar struggles. In doing so, we respect that this is their personal province, their business, their life, and their choice. We practice these rules of interpersonal etiquette with due diligence, accepting that the penalty for repeated mistakes is the loss of a friendship. However, adult children are unlikely to walk out of your life. Instead, you'll feel your children's reluctance and difficulty being around you.

It's as if all interpersonal etiquette gets tossed out the window when interacting with adult children. We get stuck on a parenting mode that necessitated a higher level of control and involvement long ago. We did have more control and opinion over our children's activities when they were young. But as they age, we needed to erect emotional boundaries crossed only with the permission of our maturing child.

Are our children not adults also? Don't they deserve the same protection that comes from the practice of good boundaries and sensitive observation?

Your assignment is about giving your relationships with your adult children every possible chance to unfold into a friendship. The tool is the same for any friendship. That is, its development is predicated on respecting boundaries, accepting differences, and dissolving your former role as parents. Use your friendships as a model to help guide you to know if a topic or question is appropriate.

Be patient and respectful. In time, you'll see your children discover the person who happens to be their parent. These children rarely stray far. Indeed, they nest nearby for years of family gatherings they sincerely want to be part of.

Lyndsey Ends Her Childhood

Lyndsey was tired of feeling inadequate and intruded upon by her parents. She sought therapy after a Christmas visit with her parents resulted in her feeling depressed and unsure of herself. It was time to mobilize the assertiveness that she drew on at work and in her day-to-day interactions.

Lyndsey was concerned about her parents' reaction to her setting limits. She anticipated Mom's guilt and Dad's anger and criticism. In therapy, we had to prepare her for each one of these by role-playing her response to her parents. Since she was in contact with her parents several times a month, we planned how she might change her relationship during one of the numerous telephone calls.

Her mom provided the first opportunity. This phone discussion unfolded as we had predicted and practiced.

LYNDSEY: Hello, Hi, Mom.

MOM: Hi, honey. How's my little girl?

LYNDSEY: I am fine, Mom.

MOM: Your dad and I cut out an article on personal safety. It's a good article on how to protect yourself when you're in public and what to do when you are home alone. Did you have the alarm service activated in your apartment? You know how important it is. Dad and I don't want to have to worry about you. We're getting too old to have to worry about things like that.

LYNDSEY: Mom, would you stop? I don't need to hear this.

MOM: I am only trying to help. Every time I try to help you, you don't appreciate it.

LYNDSEY: Well, I don't appreciate it. I don't need or want the advice.

MOM: I can't believe you are talking to your mother that way.

LYNDSEY: Mom, I'm not your little girl anymore and I don't want the constant advice or comments.

MOM: Fine, I won't say anything to you anymore.

LYNDSEY: Oh, Mom, stop. I love you, but I want the advice and comments about my personal life to stop. You think about what I said. I've got to go. I'll call you later this week. Goodbye, Mom.

Lyndsey did call later that week. She began the conversation with, "Did you think about what I said on Sunday?" Her mom acted hurt and depressed. Lyndsey repeated her expectation of no further advice or comments about her personal life. She didn't allow her mom to challenge her or respond to the guilt she put out. Lyndsey again ended the conversation with a promise to call back. Through more conversations, her mom gradually let go of her pain, but remained much more cautious about giving unsolicited advice.

The conversation with her dad followed the same pattern. However, her dad became much more angry, as she predicted. He wouldn't talk to her for almost a month. Lyndsey didn't give in to this emotional blackmail and told her mom, "When he's ready to talk, he'll talk." Her dad did love her and was able to put aside his anger and pain. In her first discussion with him in a month, Lyndsey reiterated what she said with her mom. "Dad, do you understand why I no longer want advice or comments about my personal life?" Her father didn't really want to get into it again and he answered yes without further comment.

Lyndsey was delighted with the changes in her relationship with her parents and wished she'd done it ten years earlier. We touched on how her parents also must feel a sense of relief knowing she was indeed strong and able to take care of herself. The Christmas that followed the termination of her therapy, she sent me a holiday card. In it was a brief note that she was going to visit her parents, and she wasn't dreading the visit. She had underlined the word "wasn't." Congratulations, Lyndsey.

A foolish consistency is the hobgoblin of the little mind.

RALPH WALDO EMERSON (1803–1882), SELF RELIANCE

27

Underachieving Adult Children

Her 55-year-old frame creaked as she bent over to pick up her son's shoes. One sock was two steps away, followed by another a few hops down the hallway. She managed to snag a soda can and empty pretzel bag with her free hand. She'd be back to put away the VCR tape and three remote controls, close the entertainment center, fold the afghan, open the shades, and throw out yesterday's newspaper.

When she reached the top of the stairs, she could hear her 32-year-old son snoring through the closed doors. She dropped his shoes on the floor just beneath a digital alarm clock that blared 10:52 AM. Jason stirred as the thud penetrated his sleep. She heard him plaintively asked, "What time is it?"

Jason was back living at home after a sequence of failures. Jason had dropped out of college after two-and-a-half semesters, long before moving home. He was already on academic probation and the dean was poised to throw him out if he didn't complete the third semester. His dad insisted that he work and got him a job at his company. This job could have led to advancement if Jason had been ambitious and self-directed. But the combination of chronic lateness and use of sick time, all wrapped in an endless train of excuses, got Jason fired in three months.

Even at age 21, Jason was going nowhere. His options seemed limited. Knowing he was depressed, his parents felt like it was "kicking him when he was down" to throw Jason out of the family home (as friends of theirs did with their son). They brought him to a psychiatrist who put him on an antidepressant. As instructed by the psychiatrist, Jason's parents contracted with him to either go back to school or to get a job. They loved him and assured him they would support him. Jason did stints in sales, service, and deliveries, all lasting between three and 13 months. His parents continued to worry.

When he fell in love with Rebecca, an ambitious, determined woman who was one year his senior, his mom and dad's hopes were renewed. Their spirits soared as they welcomed Rebecca into their home. They quietly hoped her self-discipline would rub off on Jason. Two and one half years later, Rebecca and Jason got married after she threatened to leave him if he didn't set a wedding date.

Marriage seemed to be good for Jason, his parents concluded. With Rebecca's help, he held steady employment, he dressed and looked better, they had their own home where their much loved daughter-in-law hosted occasional Sunday brunches and holiday meals for the family. But all of this was wearing on Rebecca, who gradually began to realize she was in this alone. She became exhausted from pursuing her own ambitious goals, all undertaken while propping up Jason. This insight exploded when she was pronounced pregnant by her OB/GYN. One month later, she terminated the pregnancy and filed for divorce. After the divorce, a depressed Jason moved back home.

Impact of Indulgence

The communities I practice in can be described as middle and upper middle socioeconomic class sprinkled with enclaves of the financially wealthy. I rarely see a family that could be described as negligent, uninvolved, or detached. I don't dispute that they exist because they do. However, in these communities, I see more of the deleterious impact of indulgence than I see from neglect. Perhaps it's because uninvolved or neglectful parents don't seek therapy, a colleague of mine remarked. I suspect this is true.

We've heard the label "latch-key kid." It conjures up images of young children unsupervised, abandoned, and fending for themselves. However, if the guilt-ridden parent comes home two hours after the children arrive and indulges them in a barrage of overcompensation, instruction, love, and junk, then they're not neglected. Despite their arrival home to an empty house, they are really indulged children. Indeed, anyone can be indulgent with their children: dads working full-time jobs, moms or dads who work at home full-time, mom and dads who work outside of the home full-time, or moms and dads who work part time.

Having Poor Boundaries

Indulgence is about a parent who has poor boundaries. When looked at closely, it can entail parents who are uncomfortable with their dual roles as nurturers and disciplinarians. In therapy, I see it in the grimaces of parents as they think about watching their children need something that isn't immediately forthcoming. These parents instantly conclude they're failing to complete their most basic role as providers. "They love well but not wisely" to quote Shakespeare.

In previous chapters, we discussed the value of the struggle and how it builds perseverance and emotional resiliency. Ideally, this begins in early childhood. These opportunities are recognized by discerning parents as the years pass and the child grows. But these opportunities were missed by Jason's parents, which brings us to the topic of this chapter: dealing with an underachieving adult child.

Directionless at Age 20

This section makes recommendations for *18-to-25-year-old* young adults who recently completed high school or some college. If this fits your child or someone you know, the following will sound familiar.

Typically, their academic performance has been marginal because of struggling with their lack of focus and self-discipline for several years. They continue to make noise about educational or employment goals that never come to fruition. As parents, what should you do?

Getting an Education

In the area of education, stop pushing. Even if they enroll in school, they're likely attending for the wrong reasons. After all, your years of encouragement and cajoling have produced very little. Give every indication that you're washing your hands of the whole matter. At a meeting with both parents present, your assignment is to tell your children something like this: "Our goals for you included an education but perhaps yours don't. Good luck. We love you and we believe in you. If education is anything you ever want, and you want us to invest *our money*, then you'll have to show us one semester of grades at a 2.5 grade point average. By the way, we will not pay for this first semester of grades. If you never want to go to school, that's OK also. There have been very successful people who dropped out of school—including Albert Einstein and Bill Gates."

The goal here is to create a boundary between your goals for your children and their own goals. Many times, underachieving adults don't know what they want because of well-intentioned parents who didn't let them develop their own volition and direction. If you deliver the message above in a convincing fashion, what frequently surfaces (eventually) is your child's ownership of a goal that has only been yours until then.

What frequently drives this ownership? Anxiety. Anxiety that forces adult children to consider what indeed is best for them and their future. In effect, you are kicking out from beneath them unnecessary emotional support that has only made them dependent and directionless.

It's critical that both parents be present and in agreement when presenting the above declaration of your emancipation from parenting. Don't give in if your son or daughter throws a fit, acts indifferently, pleads, or threatens you.

You might ask yourselves, "How are they supposed to demonstrate a semester of good grades if we don't pay for their schooling?" They can attend a relatively low-cost community college. Even if they have to take a semester or two off from school to work and save money to pay for tuition and books, so be it. Far more important than their formal education is their absolute necessity to sever their overdependence on you, to improve their self discipline, and to find a direction. Without this, a formal education is almost worthless.

Living at Home

It's rarely advisable to allow an adult child to live at home for significant time periods without paying room and board. A partial exception may be an adult child attending college full time and doing well. (If at all possible, I recommend children go away to college.) However, even these young adults should have the minimal GPA standard for parents to invest *their* money. They should also be required to work during summer breaks. Furthermore, they should be required to contribute a reasonable but significant amount toward their education. Any attendance at school that's less than full time should kick in a pro-rated requirement to pay room and board.

How much room and board they pay depends on jobs available to them. I suggest taking their gross pay and charging 50 percent of that amount. This should be delivered free of sermonizing or guilt-driven justifications. Simply state the following: "If you would like to continue to live here, then we expect $_____ in rent. If not, good luck to you. We believe in you."

Don't get pulled into lengthy explanations of how you are doing it for their own good. To explain all this is to resume the overinvolvement that contributed to your child's underachievement in the first place. Have courage. Spouses need to look for support in each other while this is unfolding. I know this isn't easy, but the potential results are worth it. Be careful what you say and keep it simple. The only response you should make back would sound like this: "That's the deal we're offering you. We understand that you may not want to take it. That's OK. We love you and believe in you."

If they find another living arrangement, so be it. You must be prepared for them to take this option. Even though you know you'll worry about their ability to make it on their own, do it anyway. There's nothing like real-world experience to jump-start directionless adult children. Furthermore, if they actually move out, this is a desirable although rare outcome to the intervention described above. They're frequently too afraid to be on their own. Thus, if they elect to move out as a result of the room and board requirement or anytime later during this process, then celebrate the turn of good fortune.

Why celebrate? In effect, your son or daughter has just taken a big step in achieving independence, which can feel unpleasant for you as parents. Still, ignore any threats they make (such as you'll never see them again) and stick with your plan.

> ***They love well but not wisely.***
> SHAKESPEARE

30 Years Old and Directionless

This section makes recommendations for parents of the *26-year-old and older adults*—the group that Jason is in. These children are overly dependent and falling behind socially and emotionally. They may have developed alcohol or drug-related problems or been through a failed marriage like Jason. Either way, the intervention needs to be decisive and strong.

The goal is essentially the same as with adult children who are younger but with certain modifications. If your adult children have addictions of any type, they should be addressed as detailed below. Once they are free of significant substance usage, then it's time to get them out and living on their own.

Set a date they have to be out by and stick to it. It can be as short as two weeks (especially if they already have a job) or as long as three months, but get them out. The conversation should go like this, with both parents present and in agreement: "We have both decided we'd like you to move out by month/day/year. Let us know if you need any help. We love and believe in you."

Don't preface the above statement with "you need to get a job first to be able to get a place on your own." This is giving them control and an opportunity they'll likely take to continue their dependence. That could unfold in passive aggressive behavior you're all too familiar with and they'll never get a job. *What will motivate them to get a job is the dawning reality that they are on their own.* Therefore, summon up all the courage you can find and set a move-out date less than the three months out. Thirty days is frequently achievable in these situations.

There's a distinct possibility—even a probability in some situations—that they're not going to take any steps whatsoever to move out in 30 days. At this point, you'll be confronted with the distasteful need to insist they move out. If you have to, literally throw them out once the spoken date arrives. You might have to put their belongings on the doorstep, but do it. I have seen situations in which parents had to call the police to evict an abusive adult child during this intervention.

Whatever it takes, do it. Remember the larger picture; you are fighting for your child's mental health, *not* abandoning him or her. If you remain overtly steadfast and determined, the message they hear is that you believe in them.

Dealing with Addictions

In my experience, underachieving, chronically dependent adult children are more prone to addictions than others. They may turn to alcohol, marihuana, cocaine, PCP, heroin, painkillers, and more. Marijuana is rarely physically addicting, although it seems to have some correlation with chronic underachievement. Abusive drinking can lead to physical addiction and, if it does, it qualifies for the exception stated below.

Addicted adult children first need to be given a chance to cope with their problem. However, continued living at home should be contingent on their getting treatment such as a 12-step program and individual or group therapy. The burden of proof of their participation in their recovery should rest on them. Treatment success needs to be verified with mandatory drug testing that's random and supervised. Make it clear to them that a positive drug test means they must move out immediately.

Remember, you're likely better off allowing adult children to bottom out than enabling them to practice their addictive behaviors year after year. I know this takes courage and you'll have moments of doubt that will haunt you, but do it anyway.

Financial Boundaries

Financial assistance to help them move out should be limited and certainly *not* ongoing. Allow them to live within their means. This gives them the opportunity to dream of the possibilities and then gradually make them happen. The struggle to making their dreams a reality is what helps them grow.

Indeed, your inability to tolerate your child struggling through the years could be the very reason you've ended up with a dependent adult child. So spend your money on yourself. Let your child scale back to renting a room from someone in a so-so neighborhood. Don't be rescuers, especially when it's clear your child has been financially irresponsible.

Down the road, when adult children have a track record of holding a job, paying their bills, establishing and maintaining credit, and improving their living arrangements, then things can be different. When they ask for a cosignatory on a car loan or help with a down payment on a condo or house that makes financial sense, then you can assist without suffering the debilitating side effects you never intended. But they must first demonstrate their ability to be independent.

Is Therapy Needed?

It may seem unusual that a clinical psychologist isn't immediately recommending psychotherapy for an adult child like Jason who is depressed. In my own practice, I prefer to meet with the parents, even if I'm going to do short-term psychotherapy with their son or daughter. The goal of my work with the parents is to get them to understand what happened and how they unintentionally developed a dependent adult child. We also look for ways to promote their adult child's independence short of having them move out.

I will treat the adult children if they are motivated, but I usually commit to only one session to assess how useful this intervention will be. In many instances, it's a waste of time and money to keep a stuck child in long-term therapy. The one hour a week I spend with this person to rally any initiative is no match for the other 167 hours a week the parents continue to indulge them and feed the illusion of not having to assume personal responsibility for their lives.

I highly recommend you find a therapist to help you with this intervention with your dependent adult child. Make sure your therapist doesn't solely focus on your adult child's depression but rather, works with you along this path. Verify the therapist has training in family therapy and be careful of paraprofessional groups who can't assess the appropriateness of the kind of intervention described above.

Jason's Epilogue

It's been several years since I've had contact with Jason or his family. At that time, he was still living at home, only sporadically dating, working part-time in a fast food restaurant and becoming increasingly depressed. Throughout his treatment, I tried in vain to get his parents to implement the plan stated above. They grieved for Jason's struggle and resisted following through with putting him out when they briefly had the courage to set a date for moving out.

A large part of Jason's parents' intentions were indeed directed at the welfare of their son and the challenges he faced. However, I suspected other underlying issues. Specifically, I was unable to get Jason's mother to realize her fear around moving beyond her role as mother and having to be alone with Jason's father. I believe the father shared this fear. They both acted from unconscious motives to keep Jason stuck because their marriage wasn't strong and parenting was the most significant activity they shared.

Both of them adamantly denied it when I attempted to raise this issue. Their inability to discuss and work on any part of their marital relationship or lives that didn't involve Jason made this a conspicuous issue I could never successfully process during therapy. It's indeed possible I was totally wrong with this diagnostic hypothesis. Jason's situation never improved. But the fact remains that Jason's life is handicapped by well-intentioned parents, his own lack of courage, and an ineffectual therapist.

Of course, Jason still can improve his life whenever he's ready. As a psychologist, this ever-present possibility helps me maintain optimism and hope in a variety of difficult therapeutic encounters. Jason can do this by confronting his fear of being alone and giving up his fantasy that others will always be there to make decisions and keep him focused. If he doesn't do this on his own, it might just happen for him when one or both of his parents pass away. I've seen adult children who have spent years as chronic underachievers finally make significant gains when their parents die. Unfortunately, one or both parents never get to see their adult child ending up OK.

I hope this isn't the situation for Jason and his family. If it is, I hope that Jason returns to therapy with me during this time of loss. I would love to witness this man's transformation into adulthood that his parents had always hoped for.

Part 5: Conclusion

The great enemy of truth is very often not the lie—
deliberate, contrived, and dishonest—
but the myth—persistent, persuasive and realistic.
Too often we hold fast to the clichés of our forebears.

JOHN F. KENNEDY, 1962 YALE COMMENCEMENT ADDRESS

28

⚮

Parting Thoughts

Every day behind closed doors, the people I counsel will share things about life, living and themselves that will prove to be of value to many. I'll continue to jot them down in the burgundy notebook next to my chair that I hope to share with you in the near future. I have found that the overwhelming majority of people are more than happy to share their stories, especially if it can help someone else. Thank you for your generosity and rescuing the very best of all your insights and stories from the shredder that erases them after seven years. Although it's time to bring an end to these stories, I wanted to leave you with a few parting thoughts.

> *Our enlightenment...is slowly building a collective wisdom that will someday transform the world where parochial interests, fear, and mistrust will subside.*

The majority of people surrounding you want you to succeed. I remind you of this to suggest that even though you may feel alone on your life path, people along the way are there for you in small and big ways. Stay open to this help and remember Jane's lesson in "Attractive Dependency" in which she learned to signal other people that occasionally she needed their support and cooperation.

Secondly, allow yourself to feel gratitude, initiated by giving thanks to people. Feeling gratitude requires you to remember what's been given to you and thus completes your process of receiving. Giving thanks to those who wanted you to succeed completes the circle of give and take. It allows those who helped along the way the satisfaction and opportunity to celebrate your success.

Although at times our issues seem complicated and overwhelming, they are not. Remember, when we're lost in the thicket of confusion and doubt, others can see our path out of the woods with much more clarity and perspective than we can. The clarity of this path is echoed in the words of my old professor, with his gesturing finger, his bushy eyebrows and black-rimmed glasses encasing his blue eyes. He said, "The issues of life are not many, the manifestations are... (many and complex)."

He implored us to look past complex issues for the basic needs. To feel secure, to feel love, to know ourselves, to have purpose, to understand, to make sense of our feelings. Our basic needs are quite simple. Their manifestation—for example, someone pursuing wealth beyond the need to attain financial security—is frequently about a need to feel loved. There are easier and more successful ways of fulfilling this need to feel loved. Although the manifestations of basic human needs can be complex, the underlying motivation is simple and uniquely human. Make sure the path you're on leads directly toward fulfilling these basic needs.

Embrace change as your journey proceeds. Most psychologists tell you that people get into trouble because they will *not* change rather than because they *have* changed. More often than not, the people I've worked with already knew the answers to their questions and the path they needed to travel. They often wanted confirmation and support while implementing their changes. Admittedly, the anticipation of change can be worrisome. Remember, however, we're trying to head off as many apocalyptic transformations as possible.

In ascending order, as we age, we must change by:

Learning how to become our own person.

Learning how to have a vocation.

Learning how to be married.

Learning how to be a parent.

Learning how to become our adult child's friend.

Learning a new direction after parenting is finished.

Learning a new direction after our careers are over.

Learning how to be elderly.

Learning how to let go, say goodbye, and die.

Embrace change. As Joseph Campbell implores, "Find direction by following your bliss." If you learn to embrace change, the path need never become permanently boring, meaningless, or lonely. Expect change, learn to transform yourself, and transcend.

At any given time, it's easy to believe we are degenerating as a people as evidenced by horrific events or disturbing cultural trends. Events like 9/11 are indeed horrific. Nevertheless, I don't believe we're degenerating as a people. From "The Evening News" we're reminded that, for every tragedy at any given time, thousands of acts of kindness and heroism take place. This proved true in the aftermath of 9/11 when a tragedy spawned thousands of acts of kindness and heroism among the people of New York. In a larger context, don't forget, we are making progress; each of our experiences teaches us lessons in living, new possibilities, deeper understanding.

Our enlightenment, if you will, is slowly building a collective wisdom that will someday transform the world where parochial interests, fear, and mistrust will subside. At some future time—a time whose foundation is being laid today—we will act cooperatively as a world culture in the noblest endeavors. Fewer resources will be squandered on the security and military necessities required today. This is all down the road.

Today, we live in a millennium in which we have only begun to talk with each other. Only in the last few moments of man's existence on this planet has mass communication been possible. This exposure to ideas and information is unparalleled in human existence. As we deepen our understanding of each other and we've fulfilled the basic needs of everyone on the planet, we will share aspects of a universal vision of living life with purpose and meaning. Do not allow the setbacks and struggles to dampen your faith. Our progress as a people mirrors our progress as individuals—with fits and starts along the way.

Don't wait for the world to change or the people around you to grow. Find peace in this world by looking within. "Finding Peace" was what Ben found in a hypnotic moment that led to his ability to live in the present. This becomes increasingly possible when we don't taint our goal-setting with the unrealistic pursuit of happiness. We learn that "Contentment" is the staple of well being. Similarly, in marriage, we accept that *commitment* is constant, not love. Rebecca learned to give-up the "Golden Fantasy" and prevented a "Romantic Ideal that Hurts." We can be challenged to let go of the myth of star-crossed lovers, which was the wish behind Robert Kinkaid's passionate but false warning to Francesca: *A love like this comes along only once in a lifetime.*

The reality of marriage can be mundane although its benefits can be enormous. Learn how to be friends, how to problem-solve, how to parent well. Know why you are together. These create the "Relationships that Work." In reality, no one is getting the ideal dream. Find peace and acceptance. Don't allow a false ideal to contaminate your ability to feel contentment.

As parents, we embrace our roles as both nurturers and disciplinarians. Ken and Maureen set the foundation for their daughter by establishing a ritual with boundaries in "Bedtime for Infants and Children." Mrs. Greene stopped begging for Zach's (and her mother's) love. She replaced it with silence and assertion as needed.

As parents, we must have the courage to allow our children the consequences of their choices. We need to appreciate just how formative the struggle becomes in developing persistence and resilience in our children. And finally, we must avoid pushing our adult children away, as Lyndsey's and too many other parents did—their children, motivated by guilt and duty, only reluctantly returning home.

Stay open to learn. Set a gentle pace as you walk a path worthy of your time.

And be well.

Thomas A. Habib, Ph.D.
Carlsbad, California
September, 2003

References and Resources

AAA Foundation for Traffic Safety, 1440 New York Avenue, N.W., Suite 201 Washington, D.C. 20005

Campbell, Joseph. *The Power of Myth,* Doubleday, New York, 1988.

Ellis, Havelock. *Studies in the Psychology of Sex, Vol 1,* Random House, 1936.

Epstein, Mark. *Thoughts Without A Thinker,* Basic Books, New York, 1995.

Evans, Nicholas. *The Horse Whisperer,* Delacorte Press, New York, 1995.

Farrell, Warren. *Why Men Are The Way They Are,* Berkley Publishing Group, New York, 1988.

Farrell, Warren. *The Myth of Male Power,* Simon and Schuster, Inc., 1993.

Goleman, Daniel. *Emotional Intelligence,* Bantam Books, New York, 1995.

Goleman, Daniel. *Working with Emotional Intelligence,* Bantam Books New York, 1998.

Hendrix, Harville. *Getting the Love You Want,* Henry Holt and Company, Inc., 1988.

Kabat-Zinn, Jon. *Wherever You Go There You Are,* Hyperion, New York, 1994.

Kaplan, Helen Singer. *The New Sex Therapy,* Brunner/Mazel, Inc. New York, 1981.

Keller, Helen. *The Open Door,* Doubleday & Company, Inc., 1957.

Masters, William H., Johnson, Virginia E. *Human Sexual Inadequacy,* Boston: Little, Brown and Company, 1970.

Mulock Craik, Dinah Maria. *A Life for a Life,* N.Y. Microform, 1877.

National Highway Traffic Safety Administration, 400 7th Street, S.W. Washington, D.C. 20590

Schnarch, David M. *Constructing the Sexual Crucible,* W.W. Norton & Company, Inc., 1991.

Schopenhauer c.f. Wampold, B. et.al. *Journal of Counseling Psychology,* Vol. 48, No. 3, 2001.

Sears, William. *Keys to Calming the Fussy Baby,* Barron's Educational Series, Inc., 1991.

Seligman, Martin E. *The Optimistic Child: A Proven Program to Safeguard Children Against Depression and Build Lifelong Resilience,* Harper Trade, 1996.

Shanor, Karen. *The Shanor Study: The Sexual Sensitivity of the American Male,* New York, Dial Press, 1978.

Thevenin, Tine. *The Family Bed: An Age Old Concept in Child Rearing,* Avery Publishing Group Wayne, New Jersey, 1987.

Watts, Alan W. *The Way of the Zen,* Pantheon Books, New York, 1957.

About the Author

Thomas A. Habib, Ph.D., is a clinical psychologist practicing in San Juan Capistrano, California. He is the founder and senior partner at Mission Psychological Consultants, Inc., a practice of clinical psychologists, psychiatrists, marital and family therapists, and interns. Known throughout the Orange County area for his work in couples' therapy, he's helped many couples strengthen and renew their struggling relationships.

Dr. Habib has become well known among pediatricians and school administrators for helping families nurture children to have confidence and volition. He has been frequently interviewed by media representatives on the ideas presented in *If These Walls Could Talk*. A keynote speaker, he presents lively, insightful programs about relationships in both home and work environments.

Dr. Habib resides in Carlsbad, California, with his wife and two daughters. His wife Christine Baser, RN, Ph.D., is a neuropsychologist specializing in head injury and rehabilitation. They have two daughters, Alexis and Adrienne. The younger one, Alexis, loves large social gatherings and is always eager to makes friends of all ages. The older one, Adrienne, has begun to muse about being raised by two psychologists.

Dr. Habib was born and raised in Worcester, Massachusetts, where he frequently returns to visit his seven brothers and sisters, and other friends and family.

Index

Order Form

Please send _____ **copies of** *If These Walls Could Talk* **@ $29.95 ea.**

Postal Orders:

> Conifer Publishing
> P.O. Box 131141
> La Costa, CA 92013

Online: www.mpccares.com/talkingwalls

Email: ConiferPub@aol.com

Telephone: (949) 248-7411, Ext. 101

Send to:

Name: _____

Address: _____

City: _____

State: _____ Zip: _____ Telephone: (   ) _____

This book is a gift from _____

Indicated in mailing package

Sales Tax:
  Add 7.75% ($2.32) for each book shipped to California addresses.

Shipping:
  $4.00 for the first book and $2.00 for each additional book.

Total cost of books $	_____
Sales tax	_____
Shipping	_____
TOTAL **$**	_____

Payment:

Check _____

Credit Card: ☐ VISA   ☐ Master Card   ☐ AMEX   ☐ Discover

Card Number: _____

Name on Card: _____ Exp. Date _____ / _____

Phone Number of Cardholder: _____

Please allow two weeks for delivery.